BUSINESS ISSUES, COMPETITION AND ENTREPRENEURSHIP

THE PATENT SYSTEM

KEY DEVELOPMENTS AND ISSUES FOR FURTHER CONSIDERATION

BUSINESS ISSUES, COMPETITION AND ENTREPRENEURSHIP

Additional books in this series can be found on Nova's website under the Series tab.

Additional e-books in this series can be found on Nova's website under the e-book tab.

BUSINESS ISSUES, COMPETITION AND ENTREPRENEURSHIP

THE PATENT SYSTEM

KEY DEVELOPMENTS AND ISSUES FOR FURTHER CONSIDERATION

DEANNA HOFFMAN
EDITOR

nova publishers
New York

Library of Congress Cataloging-in-Publication Data

ISBN: 978-1-63482-267-1

Published by Nova Science Publishers, Inc. † New York

CONTENTS

PREFACE

This book discusses the changes made as well was key developments and issues for further consideration in the patent system.

Chapter 1 - Following several years of legislative discussion concerning patent reform, the Congress enacted P.L. 112-29, signed into law on September 16, 2011. The Leahy-Smith America Invents Act, or "AIA," made significant changes to the patent system, including:

- *First-Inventor-to-File Priority System.* The AIA shifted the U.S. patent priority rule from a "first-to-invent" system to the "first-inventor-to-file principle" while allowing for a one-year grace period.
- *Prior User Rights.* The legislation established an infringement defense based upon an accused infringer's prior commercial use of an invention patented by another.
- *Assignee Filing.* Under the AIA, a patent application may be filed by the inventor's employer or other entity to which rights in the invention are assigned.
- *Post-Grant Review Proceedings.* The AIA changed the current system of administrative patent challenges at the U.S. Patent and Trademark Office (USPTO) by establishing post-grant review, *inter partes* review, and a transitional program for business method patents.
- *Public Participation in USPTO Procedures.* The legislation allowed members of the public to submit pertinent information to the USPTO concerning particular applications both before and after patent issuance.
- *USPTO Fees.* The AIA stipulated fees for USPTO patent services and allows the agency to adjust the fees in order to cover its costs. It also

required that fees collected above the amount provided for in the appropriations process be used only for the USPTO.

- *Patent Marking*. The AIA limited lawsuits challenging patent owners with false patent marking and allowed for virtual, Internet-based marking.
- *Patentable Subject Matter*. The AIA prevented patents claiming or encompassing human organisms and limited the availability of patents claiming tax strategies.
- *Best Mode*. The statute maintained the requirement that patents describe the best mode, or superior way for practicing the claimed invention, but eliminated failures to do so as a basis for invalidating the patent.

The AIA introduced a number of additional changes to the patent law, including changes to the venue and joinder statutes, the introduction of supplemental examination, and a clarification of the law of willful infringement.

Although the AIA arguably made the most significant changes to the U.S. patent statute since the 19th century, the legislation did not reflect all of the issues that were the subject of congressional discussion including the assessment of damages during infringement litigation and the publication of all pending patent applications prior to grant.

Chapter 2 - The term "compulsory license" refers to the grant of permission for an enterprise seeking to use another's intellectual property without the consent of its proprietor. The grant of a compulsory patent license typically requires the sanction of a governmental entity and provides for compensation to the patent owner. Compulsory licenses in the patent system most often relate to pharmaceuticals and other inventions pertaining to public health, but they potentially apply to any patented invention.

U.S. law allows for the issuance of compulsory licenses in a number of circumstances, and also allows for circumstances that are arguably akin to a compulsory license. The Atomic Energy Act, Clean Air Act, and Plant Variety Protection Act provide for compulsory licensing, although these provisions have been used infrequently at best. The Bayh-Dole Act offers the federal government "march-in rights," although these have not been invoked in the three decades since that legislation has been enacted. 28 U.S.C. Section 1498 provides the U.S. government with broad ability to use inventions patented by others. Compulsory licenses have also been awarded as a remedy for antitrust violations. Finally, a court may decline to award an injunction in favor of a prevailing patent owner during infringement litigation, an outcome that some observers believe is akin to the grant of a compulsory license.

A number of international agreements to which the United States and its trading partners are signatories, including the Paris Convention for the Protection of Industrial Property, World Trade Organization agreements, and certain free trade agreements, address compulsory licensing. In contrast to the United States, the patent statutes of many other nations include general provisions that allow for the award of compulsory licenses under specified conditions. A number of U.S. trading partners, including Brazil, South Africa, and Thailand, have invoked these provisions. The March 9, 2012, decision of the Indian government to grant a compulsory license on the chemotherapy drug sorafenib has attracted controversy.

Some commentators have expressed concern that compulsory licenses substantially diminish incentives for firms to conduct research and development. Others support the grant of such licenses under certain conditions, noting that many patent-granting states suffer from poverty, dire health needs, and a lack of access to patented technologies.

Congress has previously monitored the issuance of compulsory patent licenses by U.S. trading partners and may wish to continue to do so. Legislation dating from the 109th Congress would have allowed the Secretary of Health and Human Services to declare a compulsory license on a patented invention that was needed to address a public health emergency. This legislation was not enacted and has not been reintroduced.

Chapter 3 - In the past, the U.S. courts upheld gene patents that met the criteria of patentability defined by the Patent Act. However, the practice of awarding patents on genes came under scrutiny by some scientists, legal scholars, politicians, and other experts. In June 2013, the Supreme Court ruled in *Association for Molecular Pathology v. Myriad Genetics, Inc.* that genomic DNA was ineligible for patenting under 35 U.S.C. §101 due to the "product of nature" doctrine. However, the Court adopted the view that cDNA could be patented. The *Myriad* holding attempts to provide inventors and firms with incentives to conduct R&D while recognizing that patent proprietors might obtain too much control over medical practice and future research.

Chapter 4 - Congressional interest in the patent system has been demonstrated by the enactment of the Leahy-Smith America Invents Act (AIA) in the 112th Congress. Most of the provisions of the AIA apply to any type of patented invention, whether it consists of a chemical compound, mechanical device, electrical circuit, or other technology. However, other AIA provisions are specific to particular types of inventions, including business methods, tax strategies, and human organisms. The AIA reflects the principle that, for the most part, patentable inventions are generally subject to the same statutory provisions. However, a number of exceptions exist to this concept of technological neutrality.

This blended architecture has for many years prompted inquiry into whether the patent system operates best as a uniform system that applies neutrally to all inventions, or whether it could or should be tailored to meet the specific needs of different industries. Technologies and industrial sectors arguably differ in ways salient to the patent system. Among these distinctions are the costs and risks of research and development, the availability of trade secret protection as an effective alternative to patenting, the number of patents that cover a particular product, and the patterns of patent acquisition and enforcement of firms within that sector. The patent system involves a number of parameters that could potentially be adjusted to meet the needs of individual sectors, including the speed with which applications are reviewed, the scope of exclusive rights afforded by a patent, and the term of the patent.

While some observers suggest the desirability of sector-specific patent principles, others believe them to be infeasible and unwise. They observe that legislative efforts to define particular industries may prove difficult, that attorneys may sometimes be able to draft patents artfully so as to fall within a favored category, and that U.S. industry is dynamic and resistive to a static statutory definition. In addition, U.S. membership within the World Trade Organization (WTO) may limit the ability to tailor the patent system to account for different industries and inventions, to the extent that compliance with WTO standards is desired. The WTO-administered Agreement on Trade-Related Aspects of Intellectual Property, or TRIPS Agreement, in part requires WTO member states to make patent rights available without discrimination as to the field of technology. The TRIPS Agreement admits some exceptions exist to this principle of technological neutrality, however.

Should Congress believe current circumstances to be appropriate, then no action need be taken. To the degree WTO compliance is desired, Congress could also legislate along the lines permitted by the TRIPS Agreement. Notably, although the TRIPS Agreement generally disallows discrimination with respect to technological fields, it permits distinctions on other grounds. Congress could also make use of regulatory exclusivities and other complementary intellectual property rights that the TRIPS Agreement regulates less heavily.

Chapter 5 - Congress has recently demonstrated significant ongoing interest in litigation by "patent assertion entities" (PAEs), which are colloquially known as "patent trolls" and sometimes referred to as "non-practicing entities" (NPEs). The PAE business model focuses not on developing or commercializing patented inventions but on buying and asserting patents, often against firms that have already begun using the claimed technology after developing it independently, unaware of the PAE patent. PAEs include not only freestanding businesses but patent holding subsidiaries, affiliates, and shells of operating companies that want to participate in the PAE industry and/or a new means of countering competitors. The proliferation of PAEs was among the central factors raised in support of the most recent patent reform legislation, the Leahy-Smith America Invents Act of 2011 (AIA). However, the AIA contains relatively few provisions that arguably might impact PAEs, apparently because of lively debate over what, if anything, should be done about them. In the 113th Congress, the Saving High-Tech Innovators from Egregious Legal Disputes (SHIELD) Act of 2013 (H.R. 845) has been introduced in an effort to affect the number of lawsuits filed by PAEs.

PAEs emerged alongside the burgeoning tech industry around the turn of the 21st century and gained notoriety with lawsuits claiming exclusive ownership of such ubiquitous technologies as wireless email, digital video streaming, and the interactive Web. They have had the attention of Congress, the press, and the public since at least 2006, when a successful PAE suit almost caused the shutdown of BlackBerry wireless service. Such victories in court are rare for PAEs; they lose 92 percent of merits judgments. But few cases make it that far. The vast majority of defendants settle because patent litigation is risky, disruptive, and expensive, regardless of the merits; and many PAEs set royalty demands strategically well below litigation costs to make the business decision to settle an obvious one. For most PAEs, the costs of litigating and losing are more than offset by the licensing fees they can gain by demonstrating their tenacity to future defendants.

According to one estimate, PAEs generated $29 billion in direct costs from defendants and licensees in 2011, a 400 percent increase over $7 billion in 2005, and some researchers suggest these costs are primarily deadweight, with less than 25 percent flowing to support innovation and at least that much going towards legal fees. Another study reported that 62% of all patent suits filed in 2012 were brought by PAEs. Critics assert that PAEs undermine the purposes of patent law—promoting innovation by providing incentives to invest in development and commercialization of inventions—and injure companies that play a vital role in the American economy. However, defenders of PAEs argue that they actually promote invention by adding liquidity options, managing risk, and compensating small inventors. The Federal Trade Commission and several leading scholars suggest that these benefits exist but are significantly less than the costs they impose. What remains unclear is the extent of imbalance between costs and benefits and whether Congress could recalibrate it to advance the goals of patent law while avoiding unintended consequences.

This report reviews the current debate and controversy surrounding PAEs and their effect on innovation, examines the reasons for the rise in PAE litigation, and explores the legislative options available to Congress if it decides that these are issues that should be addressed.

In: The Patent System
Editor: Deanna Hoffman
ISBN: 978-1-63482-267-1

Chapter 1

THE LEAHY-SMITH AMERICA INVENTS ACT: INNOVATION ISSUES*

John R. Thomas

SUMMARY

Following several years of legislative discussion concerning patent reform, the Congress enacted P.L. 112-29, signed into law on September 16, 2011. The Leahy-Smith America Invents Act, or "AIA," made significant changes to the patent system, including:

- *First-Inventor-to-File Priority System*. The AIA shifted the U.S. patent priority rule from a "first-to-invent" system to the "first-inventor-to-file principle" while allowing for a one-year grace period.
- *Prior User Rights*. The legislation established an infringement defense based upon an accused infringer's prior commercial use of an invention patented by another.
- *Assignee Filing*. Under the AIA, a patent application may be filed by the inventor's employer or other entity to which rights in the invention are assigned.

---

* This is an edited, reformatted and augmented version of a Congressional Research Service publication R42014, prepared for Members and Committees of Congress, dated January 15, 2014.

- *Post-Grant Review Proceedings*. The AIA changed the current system of administrative patent challenges at the U.S. Patent and Trademark Office (USPTO) by establishing post-grant review, *inter partes* review, and a transitional program for business method patents.
- *Public Participation in USPTO Procedures*. The legislation allowed members of the public to submit pertinent information to the USPTO concerning particular applications both before and after patent issuance.
- *USPTO Fees*. The AIA stipulated fees for USPTO patent services and allows the agency to adjust the fees in order to cover its costs. It also required that fees collected above the amount provided for in the appropriations process be used only for the USPTO.
- *Patent Marking*. The AIA limited lawsuits challenging patent owners with false patent marking and allowed for virtual, Internet-based marking.
- *Patentable Subject Matter*. The AIA prevented patents claiming or encompassing human organisms and limited the availability of patents claiming tax strategies.
- *Best Mode*. The statute maintained the requirement that patents describe the best mode, or superior way for practicing the claimed invention, but eliminated failures to do so as a basis for invalidating the patent.

The AIA introduced a number of additional changes to the patent law, including changes to the venue and joinder statutes, the introduction of supplemental examination, and a clarification of the law of willful infringement.

Although the AIA arguably made the most significant changes to the U.S. patent statute since the 19th century, the legislation did not reflect all of the issues that were the subject of congressional discussion including the assessment of damages during infringement litigation and the publication of all pending patent applications prior to grant.

INTRODUCTION

P.L. 112-29, the Leahy-Smith America Invents Act, or "AIA," arguably made the most significant changes to the patent statute since the 19th century.[1]

Among other provisions, the statute introduced into U.S. law a first-inventor-to-file priority rule, an infringement defense based upon prior commercial use, and assignee filing. The legislation prevented patents from claiming or encompassing human organisms, limited the availability of patents claiming tax strategies, and restricted the best mode requirement. The AIA also made notable reforms to administrative patent challenge proceedings at the U.S. Patent and Trademark Office (USPTO) and to the law of patent marking. Along with numerous other changes to patent laws and procedures, these reforms were intended to modernize the U.S. patent system and to improve its fairness and effectiveness.

Congressional interest in patent reform was evidenced by sustained legislative activity that led to enactment of the AIA.[2] There is broad agreement that more patents are sought and enforced than ever before; that the attention paid to patents in business transactions and corporate boardrooms has dramatically increased; and that the commercial and social significance of patent grants, licenses, judgments, and settlements is at an all-time high.[3] As the United States becomes even more of a high-technology, knowledge-based economy, the importance of patents may grow even further in the future.

Most experts agree that patent ownership is an incentive to innovation, the basis for the technological advancement that contributes to economic growth. It is through the commercialization and use of new products and processes that productivity gains are made and the scope and quality of goods and services are expanded. Award of a patent is intended to stimulate the investment necessary to develop an idea and bring it to the marketplace embodied in a product or process. Patent title provides the recipient with a limited-time monopoly over the use of his discovery in exchange for the public dissemination of information contained in the patent application. This is intended to permit the inventor to receive a return on the expenditure of resources leading to the discovery but does not guarantee that the patent will generate commercial benefits. The requirement for publication of the patent is expected to stimulate additional innovation and other creative means to meet similar and expanded demands in the marketplace.

Passage of the AIA was preceded by several years of legislative debate about the current workings and future direction of the U.S. patent system. Although the discussion was wide-ranging, several points of concern were frequently mentioned. One was the recognition that differences between U.S. patent laws and global patent norms might increase the difficulty of domestic inventors in obtaining rights abroad. Another was that poor patent quality and high costs of litigating patent disputes might encourage speculation, or "trolling," by entrepreneurs that acquire and enforce patents. Congress also recognized that individuals, universities, and small entities play a role in the technological advancement and economic growth of the United States. A number of provisions of the AIA addressed these issues and concerns in different ways.

As ultimately enacted, the AIA also reflects the reality that the courts have been active in making changes to important patent law principles. Some observers believe that several court decisions addressed the same concerns that had motivated earlier legislative reform proposals, thereby obviating or reducing the need for congressional action. For example, judicial opinions issued in the past several years have addressed the availability of injunctive relief against adjudicated patent infringers,[4] the standards for deciding which venue is appropriate for conducting a patent trial,[5] and the assessment of damages in patent infringement cases.[6] As a result of these and other developments, several provisions found in predecessor versions of the AIA were not included in the final version of the statute.[7]

This study provides an overview of the AIA. It begins by offering a brief overview of the patent system. The specific components of this legislation are then identified and reviewed in greater detail. The report closes with further considerations.

PATENT SYSTEM FUNDAMENTALS

The patent system is grounded in Article I, Section 8, Clause 8 of the U.S. Constitution, which states that "The Congress Shall Have Power ... To promote the Progress of Science and useful Arts, by securing for limited Times to Authors and Inventors the exclusive Right to their respective Writings and Discoveries...." As mandated by the Patent Act of 1952,[8] U.S. patent rights do not arise automatically. Inventors must prepare and submit applications to the U.S. Patent and Trademark Office (USPTO) if they wish to obtain patent protection.[9] USPTO officials known as examiners then assess whether the application merits the award of a patent.[10] The patent acquisition process is commonly known as "prosecution."[11]

In deciding whether to approve a patent application, a USPTO examiner will consider whether the submitted application fully discloses and distinctly claims the invention.[12] In addition, the application must disclose the "best mode," or preferred way, that the applicant knows to practice the invention.[13] The examiner will also determine whether the invention itself fulfills certain substantive standards set by the patent statute. To be patentable, an invention must consist of a process, machine, manufacture, or composition of matter that is useful, novel, and nonobvious. The requirement of usefulness, or utility, is satisfied if the invention is operable and provides a tangible benefit.[14] To be judged novel, the invention must not be fully anticipated by a prior patent, publication, or other state-of-the-art knowledge that is collectively termed the "prior art."[15] A nonobvious invention must not have been readily within the ordinary skills of a competent artisan at the time the invention was made.[16]

If the USPTO allows the patent to issue, the patent proprietor obtains the right to exclude others from making, using, selling, offering to sell, or importing into the United States the patented invention.[17] Those who engage in these acts without the permission of the patentee during the term of the patent can be held liable for infringement. Adjudicated infringers may be enjoined from further infringing acts.[18] The patent statute also provides for the award of damages "adequate to compensate for the infringement, but in no event less than a reasonable royalty for the use made of the invention by the infringer."[19]

The maximum term of patent protection is ordinarily set at 20 years from the date the application is filed.[20] At the end of that period, others may employ that invention without regard to the expired patent.

Patent rights are not self-enforcing. Patentees who wish to compel others to observe their rights must commence enforcement proceedings, which most commonly consist of litigation in the federal courts. Although issued patents enjoy a presumption of validity, accused infringers may assert that a patent is invalid or unenforceable on a number of grounds.[21] The U.S. Court of Appeals for the Federal Circuit (Federal Circuit) possesses national jurisdiction over most patent appeals from the district courts.[22] The U.S. Supreme Court enjoys discretionary authority to review cases decided by the Federal Circuit.[23]

THE LEAHY-SMITH AMERICA INVENTS ACT

First Inventor to File

The AIA shifted the U.S. patent priority rule from the previous "first-to-invent" principle to the global norm of the "first-inventor-to-file" principle.[24] Within the patent law, the priority rule addresses the circumstance where two or more persons independently develop the identical or similar invention at approximately the same time. In such cases the patent law must establish a rule as to which of these inventors obtains entitlement to a patent.[25]

Prior to the enactment of the AIA, the United States was the only patent-issuing state to follow the first-to-invent rule. Under this principle, when more than one patent application was filed claiming the same invention, the patent would be awarded to the applicant who was the first inventor in fact. This conclusion would hold even if the first inventor was not the first person to file a patent application directed towards that invention.[26] Within this first-to-invent system,[27] the timing of real-world events, such as the date a chemist conceived of a new compound or a machinist constructed a new engine, is of significance.

In contrast, priority of invention under the first-inventor-to-file principle is established by the earliest effective filing date of a patent application disclosing the claiming invention.[28] Stated differently, the inventor who first files an application at the patent office is presumptively entitled to the patent. Whether or not the first inventor applicant is actually the first individual to complete the invention in the field is irrelevant. This priority system follows the first-inventor-to file principle.

A simple example illustrates the distinction between these priority rules. Suppose that Inventor A synthesizes a new chemical compound on August 1, 2012, and files a patent application on November 1, 2012, claiming that compound. Suppose further that Inventor B independently invents the same compound on September 1, 2012, and files a patent application on October 1, 2012. Inventor A would be awarded the patent under the first-to-invent rule, while Inventor B would obtain the patent under the first-inventor-to-file principle.

The first-inventor-to-file rule established by the AIA became effective on March 16, 2013; applications filed prior to that date remain subject to the earlier, first-to-invent principle. Notably, the AIA does not allow one individual to copy another's invention and then, by virtue of being the first to file a patent application, be entitled to a patent. All patent applicants must have originated the invention themselves, rather than derived it from another.[29] In order to police this requirement, the new legislation provides for "derivation proceedings" that allow the USPTO to determine which applicant is entitled to a patent on a particular invention.

Grace Period

The AIA continues to provide inventors with a one-year period to decide whether to pursue patent protection after disclosing their inventions to the public. Prior to enactment of the AIA, U.S. patent law essentially provided inventors with a one-year period to decide whether patent protection is desirable, and, if so, to prepare an application. Specified activities that occur before the "critical date"—patent parlance for the day one year before the application was filed—will prevent a patent from issuing.[30] If, for example, an entrepreneur first discloses an invention by publishing an article in a scientific journal, she knows that she has one year from the publication date in which to file a patent application. Importantly, uses, sales, and other technical disclosures by third parties will also start the one-year clock running. As a result, inventors have a broader range of concerns than merely their own activities.[31]

Suppose, for example, that an electrical engineer files a patent application claiming a new capacitor on February 1, 2010. While reviewing the application, a USPTO examiner discovers an October 1, 2008, journal article by another author disclosing the identical capacitor. Because the article was published prior to the critical date of February 1, 2009, that publication will prevent or "bar" the issuance of a patent on that capacitor.

Under the AIA, the grace period operates similarly, in essence protecting the patent positions of individuals who disclosed their inventions up to one year before they filed a patent application. The grace period also encourages early public disclosure of new inventions, placing that information before the public. The AIA provides that as of March 16, 2013, the grace period will operate as follows:

§ 102. Conditions for patentability; novelty

> (a) NOVELTY; PRIOR ART.—A person shall be entitled to a patent unless—
>
> (1) the claimed invention was patented, described in a printed publication, or in public use, on sale, or otherwise available to the public before the effective filing date of the claimed invention; ....
>
> (b) EXCEPTIONS.—
>
> (1) DISCLOSURES MADE 1 YEAR OR LESS BEFORE THE EFFECTIVE FILING DATE OF THE CLAIMED INVENTION.—A disclosure made 1 year or less before the effective filing date of a claimed invention shall not be prior art to the claimed invention under subsection (a)(1) if—
>
> (A) the disclosure was made by the inventor or joint inventor or by another who obtained the subject matter disclosed directly or indirectly from the inventor or a joint inventor; or (B) the subject matter disclosed had, before such disclosure, been publicly disclosed by the

> inventor or a joint inventor or another who obtained the subject matter disclosed directly or indirectly from the inventor or a joint inventor....

An example may clarify the operation of the grace period post-AIA. Suppose that on June 1, 2013, Inventor X publishes an article disclosing a new invention consisting of three components, A+B+C. On July 1, 2013, Inventor Y publishes an article disclosing the identical technology, A+B+C. Assume that Inventor Y did not derive the invention from Inventor X. Inventor X then files a patent application on August 1, 2013, claiming A+B+C. Under those circumstances, Inventor Y's publication would seemingly be patent-defeating under AIA §102(a)(1)—except that Inventor X's earlier publication excludes Inventor Y's work as prior art under AIA §102(b)(1)(B). As a result, Inventor X's patent application would not be barred by Inventor Y's publication.

Some observers have expressed concerns over the scope of the post-AIA grace period with respect to the patenting requirement of nonobviousness. Recall that in order to be awarded a patent, an invention must be both novel and nonobvious. A novel invention is one that differs from the state of the art, while an invention is considered to be nonobvious unless "the differences between the claimed invention and the prior art are such that the claimed invention as a whole would have been obvious before the effective filing date of the claimed invention to a person having ordinary skill in the art to which the claimed invention pertains."[32] The prior art definition provided in 35 U.S.C. §102 applies to both of these determinations. Although the grace period established by the AIA 35 U.S.C. §102(b)(1) seemingly operates straightforwardly for purposes of novelty, its scope with respect to obviousness may be less certain.

This issue is best illustrated through the use of a second example. Suppose that on June 1, 2013, Inventor X publishes an article disclosing a new invention consisting of three components, A+B+C. On July 1, 2013, Inventor Y publishes an article disclosing a highly similar technology, A+B+D. Once more, assume that Inventor Y did not derive the invention from Inventor X. Inventor X then files a patent application on August 1, 2013, claiming A+B+C. Under those circumstances, Inventor Y's publication qualifies as prior art against Inventor X's application under AIA §102(a)(1). The question is then whether Inventor X's earlier publication excludes the Inventor Y publication as prior art under AIA §102(b)(1)(B). The USPTO recently took the following view of the matter:

> The exception in 35 U.S.C. 102(b)(1)(B) applies if the "'subject matter' disclosed [in the prior art disclosure] had, before such [prior art] disclosure, been publicly disclosed by the inventor or a joint inventor * * * ." Thus, the exception in 35 U.S.C. 102(b)(1)(B) requires that the subject matter in the prior disclosure being relied upon under 35 U.S.C. 102(a) be the same "subject matter" as the subject matter publicly disclosed by the inventor before such prior art disclosure for the exception in 35 U.S.C. 102(b)(1)(B) to apply. Even if the only differences between the subject matter in the prior art disclosure that is relied upon under 35 U.S.C. 102(a) and the subject matter publicly disclosed by the inventor before such prior art disclosure are mere insubstantial changes, or only trivial or obvious variations, the exception under 35 U.S.C. 102(b)(1)(B) does not apply.[33]

Thus, under the USPTO's interpretation, Inventor Y's publication qualifies as prior art against Inventor X—possibly defeating Inventor X's application for failing to meet the nonobviousness requirement. Once more, the precise scope of the AIA grace period will likely await future judicial resolution.

Marking

The AIA introduced reforms to the legal rules governing the practice of "marking" articles with the numbers of particular patents. The U.S. patent laws have long encouraged patent proprietors that manufacture their patented inventions to notify the public of their patent rights.[34] Section 287(a) of the Patent Act of 1952 provides that patent owners should place the word "patent," or the abbreviation "pat.," along with the number of the patent, on patented goods. If the nature of the article does not allow this notice to be placed directly upon it, then a label may be placed on its packaging. This practice is commonly termed "marking."[35]

There is no absolute duty to mark. If a patent proprietor fails to mark in the specified manner, however, then it may receive damages only for infringing acts that occur after the infringer receives actual notice of infringement.[36] Filing an infringement lawsuit is considered to provide such actual notice. Less severely, a patent owner may issue a specific charge of infringement, commonly by sending a cease and desist letter to the infringer. The marking statute is said "to give patentees the proper incentive to mark their products and thus place the world on notice of the existence of the patent."[37]

The Patent Act also addressed the issue of "false marking." Section 292 prohibits marking a product with the number of another's patent, the name of another patent owner, or a patent or application number where no such patent or application exists. Prohibited marks also include the number of expired patents and patents that do not cover the marked product, provided such marks were affixed for the "purpose of deceiving the public." The Patent Act mandates a maximum fine of $500 for "every such" offense. According to the statute, "any person may sue for the penalty, in which event one-half shall go to the person suing and the other to the use of the United States."[38]

The AIA altered the Patent Act's false marking provision by stipulating that the statute may only be privately enforced by a "person who has suffered a competitive injury as a result of the violation...."[39] Damages in such cases would also be limited to those "adequate to compensate for the injury." This amendment would change previous law, which allows any private person to bring a civil action for false marking, whether or not they have been negatively affected. These provisions do not apply to the U.S. government. Under the provisions of the AIA, the U.S. government would continue to bring false marking suits without regard to competitive injury, and also would retain the ability to recover a maximum fine of $500 per each falsely marked article.

The AIA also allowed for "virtual marking." Under this proposal, the marking standard would be fulfilled if the product or its packaging included the word "patent" or the abbreviation "pat.," together with an Internet address that provided the number of the patent associated with the patented article.[40]

Prior Commercial Use Defense

The American Inventors Protection Act of 1999, P.L. 106-113, allowed an earlier commercial user of a "method of doing or conducting business" that was later patented by another to claim a defense to patent infringement in certain circumstances. The AIA expanded the range of individuals who may assert this defense in court. Even more significantly, the new legislation eliminated the restriction of the prior commercial use defense to business method patents. Under the AIA, a patent claiming any type of invention may be subject to the prior commercial user defense.

The prior commercial user defense accounts for the complex relationship between the law of trade secrets and the patent system. Trade secrecy protects individuals from misappropriation of valuable information that is useful in commerce. One reason an inventor might maintain the invention as a trade secret rather than seek patent protection is that the subject matter of the invention may not be regarded as patentable. Such inventions as customer lists or data compilations have traditionally been regarded as amenable to trade secret protection but not to patenting.[41] Inventors might also maintain trade secret protection due to ignorance of the patent system or because they believe they can keep their invention as a secret longer than the period of exclusivity granted through the patent system.[42]

The patent law does not favor trade secret holders, however. Well-established patent law provides that an inventor who makes a secret, commercial use of an invention for more than one year prior to filing a patent application at the USPTO forfeits his own right to a patent.[43] This policy is based principally upon the desire to maintain the integrity of the statutorily prescribed patent term. The patent law grants patents a term of 20 years, commencing from the date a patent application is filed.[44] If the trade secret holder could make commercial use of an invention for many years before choosing to file a patent application, he could disrupt this regime by delaying the expiration date of his patent.[45]

Settled patent law principles established that prior secret uses would not defeat the patents of later inventors.[46] If an earlier inventor made secret commercial use of an invention, and another person independently invented the same technology later and obtained patent protection, then the trade secret holder could face liability for patent infringement. This policy is based upon the reasoning that once issued, published patent instruments fully inform the public about the invention, while trade secrets do not. Between a subsequent inventor who patented the invention, and thus had disclosed the invention to the public, and an earlier trade secret holder who had not, the law favored the patent holder.

An example may clarify this rather complex legal situation. Suppose that Inventor A develops and makes commercial use of a new manufacturing process. Inventor A chooses not to obtain patent protection, but rather maintains that process as a trade secret. Many years later, Inventor B independently develops the same manufacturing process and promptly files a patent application claiming that invention. In such circumstances, Inventor A's earlier, trade secret use does not prevent Inventor B from procuring a patent. Furthermore, if the USPTO approves the patent application, then Inventor A faces infringement liability should Inventor B file suit against him.

The American Inventors Protection Act of 1999 somewhat modified this principle. That statute in part provided an infringement defense for an earlier user of a "method of doing or conducting business" that was later patented by another. By limiting this defense to patented methods of doing business, Congress responded to the 1998 Federal Circuit opinion in *State Street Bank and Trust Co. v. Signature Financial Group.*[47] That judicial opinion recognized that business methods could be subject to patenting, potentially exposing individuals who had maintained business methods as trade secrets to liability for patent infringement.

Again, an example may aid understanding of the prior commercial user defense. Suppose that Inventor X develops and exploits commercially a new method of doing business. Inventor X maintains his business method as a trade secret. Many years later, Inventor Y independently develops the same business method and promptly files a patent application claiming that invention. Even following the enactment of the American Inventors Protection Act, Inventor X's earlier, trade secret use would not prevent Inventor Y from procuring a patent. However, should the USPTO approve Inventor Y's patent application, and should Inventor Y sue Inventor X for patent infringement, then Inventor X may potentially claim the benefit of the first inventor defense. If successful,[48] Inventor X would enjoy a complete defense to infringement of Inventor Y's patent.

Prior to the AIA, the prior commercial user defense could "be asserted only by the person who performed the acts necessary to establish the defense...."[49] The AIA also allowed the defense to be asserted by "any other entity that controls, is controlled by, or is under common control with such person...."[50]

In addition, the AIA eliminated the restriction of the prior commercial user defense to business method patents. As a result, any type of patented invention may be subject to the prior commercial user defense. The new legislation also exempted patents held by universities from the prior commercial user defense when it stipulates that this is not available if "the claimed invention ... was made, owned or subject to an obligation of assignment to either an institution of higher education ... or a technology transfer organization whose primary purpose is to facilitate the commercialization of technologies developed by one or more such institutions of higher education."

Inventor's Oath and Assignee Filing

As the law stood prior to enactment of the AIA, a patent application had to be filed by the inventor—that is, the natural person or persons who developed the invention.[51] This rule applied even where the invention was developed by individuals in their capacity as employees. Even though rights to the invention usually have been contractually assigned to an employer, for example, the actual inventor, rather than the employer, must be the one that applies for the patent. In particular, Section 115 of the Patent Act obliges each applicant also to submit an oath or declaration stating that he believes himself to be the "original and first inventor" of the subject matter for which he seeks a patent. Section 118 of the Patent Act allowed a few exceptions to this general rule. If an inventor cannot be located, or refuses to perform his contractual obligation to assign an invention to his employer, then the employer may file the patent application in place of the inventor.

The AIA modified these rules by incorporating the exceptions found in current Section 118 into Section 115 of the Patent Act.[52] This reform appears to be primarily technical in nature, although a few differences between the new statute and prior law exist. First, the new law requires inventors to declare only that they are the "original inventor"—rather than the "original and first inventor"—in keeping with the proposed shift to a first-inventor-to-file priority system. Second, the new law allows an "individual who is under an obligation of assignment for patent [to] include the required statements ... in the assignment executed by the individual, in lieu of filing such statements separately." This provision comports with the allowance of the filing of patent applications by employers and other assignees of patent rights.

The AIA further stipulated that a "person to whom the inventor has assigned or is under an obligation to assign the invention may make an application for patent." Individuals who otherwise make a showing of a "sufficient proprietary interest in the matter" may also apply for a patent on behalf of the inventor upon a sufficient show of proof of the pertinent facts. Under the new law, if the USPTO "Director grants a patent on an application filed under this section by a person other than the inventor, the patent shall be granted to the real party in interest and upon such notice to the inventor as the Director considers to be sufficient."

Willful Infringement/Advice of Counsel

The patent law of the United States allows a court to "increase the damages up to three times the amount found or assessed."[53] An award of enhanced damages, as well as the amount by which the damages will be increased, is committed to the discretion of the trial court. Although the statute does not specify the circumstances in which enhanced damages are appropriate, the Federal Circuit recently explained that "a patentee must show by clear and convincing evidence that the infringer acted despite an objectively high likelihood that its actions constituted infringement of a valid patent."[54] This circumstance is termed "willful infringement."[55]

Courts will not ordinarily enhance damages due to willful infringement if the adjudicated infringer did not know of the patent until charged with infringement in court, or if the infringer acted with the reasonable belief that the patent was not infringed or that it was invalid. Prior to the 2007 decision in *In re Seagate Technology*, Federal Circuit decisions emphasized the duty of someone with actual notice of a competitor's patent to exercise due care in determining if his acts will infringe that patent.[56] In *Seagate Technology*, however, the Federal Circuit opted to "abandon the affirmative duty of due care."[57] The court of appeals instead explained that "proof of willful infringement permitting enhanced damages requires at least a showing of objective recklessness."[58]

Prior to 2004, the Federal Circuit held that when an accused infringer invoked the attorney-client or work-product privilege, courts should be free to reach an adverse inference that either (1) no opinion had been obtained or (2) an opinion had been obtained and was contrary to the infringer's desire to continue practicing the patented invention.[59] However, in its decision in *Knorr-Bremse Systeme fuer Nutzfahrzeuge GmbH v. Dana Corp.*,[60] the Federal Circuit expressly overturned this principle. The Court of Appeals further stressed that the failure to obtain legal advice did not occasion an adverse inference with respect to willful infringement either. Following the *Knorr-Bremse* opinion, willful infringement determinations are based upon "the totality of circumstances, but without the evidentiary contribution or presumptive weight of an adverse inference that any opinion of counsel was or would have been unfavorable."[61]

The AIA included language specifying that the "failure of an infringer to obtain the advice of counsel ... may not be used to prove that the accused infringer willfully infringed the patent...."[62] This provision appears essentially to codify the holding of *Knorr-Bremse* described above.

Post-Grant Proceedings

The AIA made a number of changes to the post-grant review proceedings administered by the USPTO. In particular, the AIA (1) replaced the previous *inter partes* reexamination system with *inter partes* review proceedings;[63] (2) introduced a new proceeding titled "post-grant review";[64] (3) established a new supplemental examination procedure;[65] and (4) created a new transitional post-grant review proceeding for the review of the validity of certain business method patents.[66] Each of these post-grant proceedings will be reviewed in turn.

Inter Partes and Post-Grant Review

Perhaps most significantly, the AIA replaced the existing *inter partes* reexamination system with *inter partes* review proceedings[67] and introduced a new proceeding titled "post-grant review."[68] Both *inter partes* and post-grant reviews are patent revocation proceedings administered by the USPTO. They would operate similarly to the so-called "reexamination" system which has been part of U.S. law since 1981. Prior to the September 16, 2012, effective date established by the AIA, the USPTO had administered two types of reexamination proceedings, termed *ex parte* and *inter partes*.

Under the reexamination statute, any individual, including the patentee, a competitor, and even the USPTO Director, may cite a prior art patent or printed publication to the USPTO. If the USPTO determined that this reference raised a "substantial new question of patentability" with respect to an issued patent, then it would essentially reopen prosecution of the issued patent. Traditional reexamination proceedings were conducted in an accelerated fashion on an *ex parte* basis—that is to say, as a dialogue between applicant and examiner without extended participation by others. Following the American Inventors Protection Act of 1999,[69] an *inter partes* reexamination allowed the requester to participate more fully in the proceedings through the submission of arguments and the filing of appeals. Either sort of reexamination may have resulted in a certificate confirming the patentability of the original claims, an amended patent with narrower claims, or a declaration of patent invalidity.

The AIA established a new proceeding termed a "post-grant review." Unlike previous reexamination proceedings, petitioners may challenge validity based upon on any ground of patentability in a post-grant review. A post-grant review must be filed within nine months of the date of patent grant. To initiate a post-grant review, the petitioner must present information that, if not rebutted, would demonstrate that it is more likely than not that at least one of the claims is unpatentable. A post-grant review must be completed within one year of its commencement, with an extension of six months possible for good cause shown. As well, the individual who commenced the proceeding, along with his privies (people who have a legal interest in the patent), are barred in the future from raising issues that were "raised or reasonably could have been raised" during the post-grant review.

Although the AIA retained *ex parte* reexamination, it replaced the predecessor *inter partes* reexamination proceedings with a similar system termed "*inter partes* review." A notable difference between the old and new proceedings is that the USPTO will be required to complete the proceeding within one year of its commencement, with an extension of six months possible for good cause shown. In broad outline, the law allows a person who is not the patent owner to file a petition requesting *inter partes* review nine months after a patent issues or reissues, or the conclusion of any post-grant review, whichever occurs later. In contrast to the post-grant review, the basis for requesting an *inter partes* review is restricted to patents or printed publications. As a result, patent challenges under *inter partes* review are limited to the patentability issues of novelty and nonobviousness.[70] Post-grant reviews allow a patent challenger to raise additional patentability issues, such as unpatentable subject matter or lack of enablement, that are not based upon a patent or printed publication.

Under the AIA, the petitioner must demonstrate that there is a "reasonable likelihood" that he would prevail with respect to at least one claim in order for the *inter partes* proceeding to begin. Under the time frames established, the effective result is that a patent may be challenged at the USPTO on any basis of any patentability issue within nine months from the date it issued (via post-grant review). Thereafter, and throughout its entire term, the patent may be challenged at the USPTO on the grounds of novelty and nonobviousness (via *inter partes* review).

The AIA stipulated that an accused infringer may not seek *inter partes* review if he has already filed a lawsuit challenging the patent or more than six months have passed since the date the accused infringer was served with a complaint alleging infringement of that patent. The law afforded the patent proprietor a single opportunity to amend its patent during the proceeding, with further opportunities available with good cause shown. Should the patent survive the *inter partes* review proceeding, the individual who commenced the proceeding, along with his privies, are barred in the future from raising issues that were "raised or reasonably could have been raised."

Supplemental Examination

The AIA established a new post-issuance administrative proceeding termed "supplemental examination."[71] This proceeding appears to be based upon a need to address concerns over the legal doctrine of inequitable conduct, a topic that bears some explanation. The administrative process of obtaining a patent from the USPTO has traditionally been conducted as an *ex parte* procedure. Stated differently, patent prosecution involves only the applicant and the USPTO.

Members of the public, and in particular the patent applicant's marketplace competitors, do not participate in patent acquisition procedures.[72] As a result, the patent system relies to a great extent upon the applicant's observance of a duty of candor and truthfulness towards the USPTO.

An applicant's obligation to proceed in good faith may be undermined, however, by the great incentive applicants might possess not to disclose, or to misrepresent, information that might deleteriously impact their prospective patent rights. The patent law therefore penalizes those who stray from honest and forthright dealings with the USPTO. Under the doctrine of "inequitable conduct," if an applicant intentionally misrepresents a material fact or fails to disclose material information, then the resulting patent will be declared unenforceable.[73] Two elements must exist before a court will decide that the applicant has engaged in inequitable conduct. First, the patentee must have misrepresented or failed to disclose material information to the USPTO in the prosecution of the patent. Second, such nondisclosure or misrepresentation must have been intentional.[74]

To limit the use of inequitable conduct in patent litigation, the AIA permitted patent owners to request a "supplemental examination" in order to "consider, reconsider, or correct information believed to be relevant to the patent." If the USPTO Director believes that this information raises a substantial new question of patentability, then a reexamination will be ordered. The AIA provides that a "patent shall not be held unenforceable ... on the basis of conduct relating to information that had not been considered, was inadequately considered, or was incorrect in a prior examination of the patent if the information was considered, reconsidered, or corrected during a supplemental examination of the patent." The supplemental examination request and resulting reexamination must be concluded prior to the start of litigation for the patent to obtain this benefit. The statute stipulates that if there is evidence of "material fraud," the Director of the USPTO is authorized to notify the Attorney General for "such further action as the Attorney General may deem appropriate."

Transitional Program for Covered Business Method Patents

The AIA created a transitional post-grant review proceeding for the review of the validity of certain business method patents.[75] This transitional proceeding is limited to patents that claim "a method or corresponding apparatus for performing data processing operations utilized in the practice, administration, or management of a financial product or service, except that the term shall not include patents for technological inventions." Only individuals who have been either sued for infringement or charged with infringement of a business method patent may petition the USPTO to commence such a proceeding. The transitional program applies to all business method patents issued before, on, or after the date of enactment of the legislation.

The AIA stipulated that a party may seek a stay of litigation related to the transitional proceeding, and that the district court's decision may be subject to an immediate interlocutory appeal to the Federal Circuit. This transitional program is subject to a sunset provision that would repeal the program after eight years. In addition, the statute provided that its business method patent provisions shall not be construed as amending or interpreting categories of patent-eligible subject matter.

Post-Grant Citation of Prior Art

The USPTO has long allowed any person at any time to bring to the agency's attention "patents or printed publications" believed to "have a bearing on the patentability of any claim of a particular patent."[76] That person may also include a written statement explaining the relevance of the cited document to the patent. This sort of "prior art citation" does not provoke any sort of administrative proceeding. However, the USPTO will place these submissions within the official file of the relevant patent, where they are accessible to the public. Prior art that potentially has a negative impact upon the patent's validity may be of considerable interest to the patent owner, its customers and competitors, and possibly others. The name of the person who files a prior art citation may be kept confidential by request.

The ability of members of the public to cite to the USPTO information that may be pertinent to the validity of a granted patent has been augmented under the provisions of the AIA. The AIA also allowed the citation of written statements that the patent owner has filed before a federal court or the USPTO regarding the scope of the patent's claims.[77]

Preissuance Submissions

The AIA expanded the possibilities for members of the public to comment upon pending applications at the USPTO. Prior to this legislation, interested individuals could file a "protest" at the agency. Such a protest was required to identify the application specifically and be served upon the applicant. The protest had to include a copy and, if necessary, an English translation, of any patent, publication, or other information relied upon. The protester was required to explain the relevance of each item.[78]

Protest proceedings have traditionally played a small role in U.S. patent practice. Until Congress enacted the American Inventors Protection Act of 1999, the USPTO maintained applications in secrecy. Therefore, the circumstances in which members of the public would learn of the precise contents of a pending patent application were relatively limited. Following the 1999 legislation, the USPTO began to publish many pending patent applications. Seemingly aware of this possibility, the 1999 Act provided that the USPTO shall "ensure that no protest or other form of pre-issuance opposition ... may be initiated after publication of the application without the express written consent of the applicant."[79] Of course, the effect of this provision was to eliminate the possibility of protest in exactly that class of cases where the public was most likely to learn of the contents of a pending application.

Through rulemaking, the USPTO had nonetheless established a limited mechanism for members of the public to submit information they believe is pertinent to a pending, published application. The submitted information must consist of either a patent or printed publication, and it must be submitted within two months of the date the USPTO published the pending application. Nondocumentary information that may be relevant to the patentability determination, such as sales or public use of the invention, will not be considered.[80] In addition, because Congress stipulated that no protest or pre-grant opposition may occur absent the consent of the patent applicant, the USPTO had explained that it will not accept *comments* or *explanations* concerning the submitted patents or printed publications. If such comments were attached, USPTO staff would redact them before the submitted documents were forwarded to the examiner.[81]

The AIA expanded the possibility for preissuance submissions. Under the legislation, any person may submit patent documents and other printed publications to the USPTO for review. Such prior art must be submitted within the later date of either (1) the date the USPTO issues a notice of allowance to the patent applicant; or (2) either six months after the date of pre-grant publication of the application, or the date of the first rejection of any claim by the USPTO examiner. Such a submission must include “a concise description of the asserted relevance of each submitted document.”

Venue

The AIA altered the venue provisions that apply to suits where the USPTO is a party—for example, appeals from inventors whose patent applications have been rejected.[82] Such cases are currently heard by the District Court for the District of Columbia. Under the AIA, the District Court for the Eastern District of Virginia will hear such cases. This change in venue may reflect the fact that the headquarters of the USPTO is no longer located within Washington, DC, but rather in Alexandria, VA.

USPTO Fee-Setting Authority and Funding

The USPTO enjoys certain rulemaking authority provided by law. The USPTO may establish regulations that “govern the conduct of proceedings” before it, for example, as well as regulations that “govern the recognition and conduct” of patent attorneys.[83] However, the fees charged by the USTPO currently were determined by Congress.

The AIA granted the USPTO additional authority “to set or adjust by rule any fee established or charged by the Office” under certain provisions of the patent and trademark laws.[84] This provision appears to provide the USPTO with greater flexibility to adjust its fee schedule absent congressional intervention. The new law requires that “patent and trademark fee amounts are in the aggregate set to recover the estimated cost to the Office for processing, activities, services and materials relating to patents and trademarks, respectively, including proportionate shares of the administrative costs of the Office.”

The AIA additionally stipulated fees for patent services provided by the USPTO.[85] In general, the new law raises the fees slightly. For example, the fees for filing a patent application and for the issuance of an approved application were $300 and $1,400 respectively; the new fees are $330 and $1,510. As previously discussed, each of these fees would then presumably be subject to adjustment by the USPTO.

The legislation created within the Treasury a "Patent and Trademark Fee Reserve Fund" into which fee collections above that "appropriated by the Office for that fiscal year" will be placed. These funds will be available to the USPTO "to the extent and in the amounts provided in appropriations Acts" and may only be used for the work of the Office.[86]

The AIA also established a new "micro entity" category of applicants.[87] A micro entity must make a certification that it qualifies as a small entity, has not been named on five previously filed patent applications, does not have a gross income exceeding three times the average gross income, and has not conveyed an interest in the application to another entity with an income exceeding that threshold. Micro entities would be entitled to a 75% discount on many USPTO fees. The USPTO Director is given authority to limit those who qualify as a micro entity if such limitations "are reasonably necessary to avoid an undue impact on other patent applicants or owners and are otherwise reasonably necessary and appropriate." The USPTO must inform Congress at least three months in advance of imposing such limitations.

Tax Strategy Patents

In recent years, the USPTO has issued patents on financial, investment, and other methods that individuals might use in order to minimize their tax obligations.[88] Under the AIA, for the purpose of evaluating whether an invention meets the requirements of novelty and nonobviousness, "any strategy for reducing, avoiding, or deferring tax liability, whether known or unknown at the time of the invention or application for patent, shall be deemed insufficient to differentiate a claimed invention from the prior art."[89] Under this rule, unless a tax strategy patent claimed an additional component that met the novelty and nonobviouness requirements—such as new computer hardware—then the invention could not be patented. The new law stipulates that this provision does not apply to that part of an invention "used solely for preparing a tax or information return or other tax filing...."

The AIA stipulated that the tax strategy patent provision does not apply to "a method, apparatus, technology, computer program product, or system used solely for financial management, to the extent it is severable from any tax strategy or does not limit the use of any tax strategy by any taxpayer or tax adviser." The statute also stated that "[n]othing in this section shall be construed to imply that other business methods are patentable or that other business method patents are valid."

Best Mode

The U.S. patent statute requires inventors to "set forth the best mode contemplated by the inventor of carrying out his invention."[90] Failure to disclose the best mode known to the inventor is a ground for invalidating an issued patent. The courts have established a two-part standard for analyzing whether an inventor disclosed her best mode in a particular patent. The first inquiry was whether the inventor knew of a way of practicing the claimed invention that she considered superior to any other. If so, then the patent instrument must identify, and disclose sufficient information to enable persons of skill in the art to practice that best mode.[91]

The AIA continued to apply the best mode requirement to all patents. However, violation of the best mode requirement no longer forms the basis for an accused infringer's defense to a charge of patent infringement during enforcement litigation or post-grant review proceedings.[92] Compliance with the best mode requirement remains subject to review by USPTO examiners during the initial prosecution of a patent, although USPTO rejection of applications based upon failure to comply with the best mode requirement is reportedly a rare circumstance.[93]

Jurisdiction and Joinder

The AIA confirms that state courts do not possess jurisdiction to hear claims for relief under the patent, plant variety protection, and copyright laws.[94] The statute further provides that the Federal Circuit possesses jurisdiction over appeals relating to patent and plant variety protection cases. In addition, cases are allowed to be removed from courts that do not possess jurisdiction and transferred to those that do.

The AIA also stipulated that accused infringers may only be joined in a single lawsuit by the patent proprietor if the allegations of infringement arise out of "the same transaction, occurrence, or series of transactions or occurrences...."[95] Furthermore, "accused infringers may not be joined in one action as defendants ... based solely on allegations that they each have infringed the patent or patents in suit." The new joinder provision appears to prevent patent owners from suing multiple firms in one lawsuit based merely on the allegation that they infringe the same patent through similar products. The patent owner would instead have to sue each accused infringer in a separate lawsuit.

The AIA joinder statute does not apply to patent cases pursued under the auspices of the Drug Price Competition and Patent Term Restoration Act of 1984, commonly known as the Hatch-Waxman Act.[96] In addition, an accused infringer may waive the joinder limitation with respect to itself.

USPTO Satellite Offices

The USPTO has long been required to maintain its principal office in the metropolitan Washington, DC, area. The Patent Act further allowed the USPTO to "establish satellite offices in such other places in the United States as it considers necessary and appropriate in the conduct of its business."[97] The AIA required the USPTO to establish three or more additional satellite offices in the United States subject to available resources.[98] The satellite offices are intended to increase inventor outreach activities, enhance patent examiner retention, improve recruitment of patent examiners, decrease the number of unexamined patent applications, and improve the quality of patent examination. The USPTO is required to ensure the geographic diversity of its satellite offices. The AIA also designates the Detroit satellite office as the "Elijah J. McCoy United States Patent and Trademark Office."[99] The USPTO has announced that the agency would open satellite offices in Dallas, Denver, Detroit, and Silicon Valley.[100]

Other USPTO Programs

The AIA provided for other reforms relating to the USPTO. Among them is the creation of a patent ombudsman program for small business concerns, subject to available resources.[101] In addition, the legislation allowed the USPTO to prioritize examination of patent applications relating to technologies that are "important to the national economy or national competitiveness."[102] The new law proposed that studies be undertaken in the following areas: patents on genetic testing; diversity of patent applicants; international patent protection for small businesses; consequences of litigation by non-practicing entities; and implementation of the legislation.

Prohibition of Patents on Humans

The USPTO has interpreted the Thirteenth Amendment, which bans human slavery, as barring patents claiming human beings.[103] The AIA gave statutory footing to this policy by stipulating that "no patent may issue on a claim directed to or encompassing a human organism."[104]

Patent Term Extension Filings

The Drug Price Competition and Patent Term Restoration Act of 1984, commonly known as the Hatch-Waxman Act, provides holders of patents on pharmaceuticals and other regulated products with an extended term of protection to compensate for delays experienced in obtaining marketing approval. Under prior law, a petition to receive such a term extension "may only be submitted [to the USPTO] within the sixty-day period beginning on the date the product received permission under the provision of law under which the applicable regulatory review period occurred...."[105] The AIA stipulated that if regulatory approval is transmitted after 4:30 PM Eastern time on a business day, or is transmitted on a day that is not a business day, then the product shall be deemed to have received such permission on the next business day.[106]

FURTHER CONSIDERATIONS

The AIA was the product of years of discussion and debate, but some observers believe that Congress did not address certain issues of pressing concern to the patent system. One of these issues involves the propriety of current judicial assessments of damages in patent infringement cases. Some observers believe that judges and juries have tended to overcompensate patent holders when they make damages awards, particularly in cases where the accused infringement includes additional features not covered by the patent.[107] Other commentators found the level of compensation to be appropriate and expressed concerns that legislative reforms might reduce damages awards to such a degree as to diminish the value of patent ownership.[108] A number of recent judicial opinions, including *Lucent Technologies, Inc. v. Gateway, Inc.*,[109] appear to have recognized expressed concerns about damages awards in patent cases and the Federal Circuit has issued rulings designed to increase their fairness and predictability. Perhaps because of these judicial developments, the AIA ultimately did not address the award of damages in patent cases. For some, however, concerns linger concerning the damages issues.[110]

Some observers believe that Congress should have required the USPTO to publish all patent applications during their pendency. When enacting the American Inventors Protection Act of 1999, Congress for the first time introduced the concept of pre-grant publication into U.S. law. Since November 29, 2000, U.S. patent applications have been published 18 months from the date of filing, with some exceptions. The most significant of these exceptions applies where the inventor represents that he will not seek patent protection abroad. In particular, if an applicant certifies that the invention disclosed in the U.S. application will not be the subject of a patent application in another country that requires publication of applications 18 months after filing, then the USPTO will not publish the application.[111] As a result, inventors who do not wish to seek foreign patent rights retain the possibility of avoiding pre-grant publication. Congress had previously considered eliminating this exception, and some observers continue to believe this was the preferable option. On the other hand, many commentators believe that this exception is more fair to individuals, small firms, and other innovators that may be especially vulnerable to piracy of their products.

Another concern that some observers argue has not been sufficiently addressed is that of patent fee "diversion." Under that practice, the USPTO is not provided the budget authority through the appropriations process to spend all fees collected within a fiscal year. Beginning in 1990, appropriations measures have, at times, limited the ability of the agency to use the full amount of fees collected in each fiscal year. Some observers believe that "fee diversion" has limited the ability of the USPTO to discharge its statutory duties effectively. On the other hand, others believe that the agency obtains sufficient financial support and point to the need to support other governmental programs.[112] The approach embodied in the AIA keeps USPTO use of fees within the appropriations process, but mandates that any excess fees be used only to fund USPTO activities.

The AIA is by any reasonable measure a watershed event in the field of intellectual property law. The numerous reforms introduced by the legislation, intended to improve, update, and adopt global best practices, will undoubtedly bring immediate changes to patent practice by the USPTO, the private bar, and innovative firms. Experience will inform us whether the legislation meets its intended goals of increasing patent quality, making patent dispute resolution more fair and efficient, improving the environment for innovation, and enhancing the economic growth of the United States.

End Notes

[1] The AIA was subject to technical correction legislation, H.R. 6621, which was passed by the House on December 18, 2012, and the Senate on December 28, 2012. H.R. 6621 was signed by the President on January 14, 2013.

[2] See CRS Report R41638, Patent Reform in the 112th Congress: Innovation Issues, by Wendy H. Schacht and John R. Thomas; CRS Report R40481, Patent Reform in the 111th Congress: Innovation Issues, by Wendy H. Schacht and John R. Thomas; CRS Report RL33996, Patent Reform in the 110th Congress: Innovation Issues, by John R. Thomas and Wendy H. Schacht; and CRS Report RL32996, Patent Reform: Innovation Issues, by John R. Thomas and Wendy H. Schacht.

[3] Statistics from the United States Patent and Trademark Office (USPTO) support this account. In 1981, 106,413 utility patent applications were received at the U.S. Patent and Trademark Office (USPTO); by 2011, this number had increased to 503,582 applications. During the same time period, the number of U.S. utility patents granted grew from 65,771 to 224,505. U.S. Patent and Trademark Office, U.S. Patent Statistics, Calendar Years 1963-2011, available at http://www.uspto.gov/web/offices/ac/ido/oeip/taf/us_stat.pdf.

[4] eBay Inc. v. MercExchange, L.L.C., 547 U.S. 388 (2006).

[5] In re TS Tech USA Corp., 551 F.3d 1315 (Fed. Cir. 2008).

[6] Lucent Technologies, Inc. v. Gateway, Inc., 580 F.3d 1301 (Fed. Cir. 2009).

[7] See papers cited in footnote 2.

[8] P.L. 82-593, 66 Stat. 792 (codified at Title 35 United States Code).

[9] 35 U.S.C. §111.

[10] 35 U.S.C. §131.

[11] John R. Thomas, "On Preparatory Texts and Proprietary Technologies: The Place of Prosecution Histories in Patent Claim Interpretation," 47 UCLA Law Review (1999), 183.

[12] 35 U.S.C. §112.

[13] Ibid.

[14] 35 U.S.C. §101.

[15] 35 U.S.C. §102.

[16] 35 U.S.C. §103.

[17] 35 U.S.C. §271(a).

[18] 35 U.S.C. §283.

[19] 35 U.S.C. §284.

[20] 35 U.S.C. §154(a)(2). Although patent term is based upon the filing date, the patentee gains no enforceable legal rights until the USPTO allows the application to issue as a granted patent. A number of Patent Act provisions may modify the basic 20-year term, including examination delays at the USPTO and delays in obtaining marketing approval for the patented invention from other federal agencies.

[21] 35 U.S.C. §282.

[22] 28 U.S.C. §1295(a)(1).

[23] 28 U.S.C. §1254(1).

[24] P.L. 112-29 at §3(b).

[25] See Roger E. Schechter & John R. Thomas, Principles of Patent Law §1.2.5 (2d ed. 2004).

[26] In addition, the party that was the first to invent must not have abandoned, suppressed or concealed the invention. 35 U.S.C. §102(g)(2).

[27] See Charles E. Gholz, "First-to-File or First-to-Invent?," 82 Journal of the Patent and Trademark Office Society (2000), 891.

[28] See Peter A. Jackman, "Adoption of a First-to-File System: A Proposal," 26 University of Baltimore Law Review (1997), 67.

[29] 35 U.S.C. §101.

[30] 35 U.S.C. §102(b).

[31] Schechter & Thomas, supra, at §4.3.1.

[32] 35 U.S.C. §103.

[33] USPTO, Examination Guidelines for Implementing the First-Inventor-to-File Provisions of the Leahy-Smith America Invents Act, 77 Federal Register (July 26, 2012), 43759, 43762.

[34] For further discussion of current patent marking issues and proposed legislation, see CRS Report R41418, False Patent Marking: Litigation and Legislation, by Brian T. Yeh.

[35] See Schechter & Thomas, supra, at §9.2.3.

[36] It should be further appreciated that under 35 U.S.C. §286, "no recovery shall be had for any infringement committed more than six years prior to the filing of the complaint or counterclaim for infringement in the action."

[37] Laitram Corp. v. Hewlett-Packard Co., 806 F. Supp. 1294, 1296 (E.D. La. 1992).

[38] 35 U.S.C. §292(b). This sort of proceeding is termed a qui tam action.

[39] P.L. 112-29 at §16(b).

[40] P.L. 112-29 at §16(a).

[41] Restatement of Unfair Competition §39.

[42] David D. Friedman, "Some Economics of Trade Secret Law," 5 Journal of Economic Perspectives (1991), 61, 64.

[43] 35 U.S.C. §102(b). See Metallizing Engineering Co. v. Kenyon Bearing & Auto Parts, 153 F.2d 516 (2d Cir. 1946).

[44] 35 U.S.C. §154.

[45] The AIA states in part that an invention may not be patented if it was "in public use, on sale, or otherwise available to the public" anywhere in the world prior to the inventor's filing date. As noted, earlier case law had held that secret uses and sales offers could, in some circumstances, qualify as prior art as being a "public use" and "on sale" under §102(b) of the predecessor statute. Whether this law remains sound is subject to some debate. USPTO Examination Guidelines state that the "phrase 'public use' in AIA 35 U.S.C. § 102(a)(1) is treated as having the same meaning as 'in public use' in pre-AIA 35 U.S.C. § 102(b)." However, some legislative history of the AIA suggests that the rules might have changed. For example, during one debate Senator Kyl stated:

Public uses and sales of an invention will remain prior art, but only if they make the invention available to the public. An inventor's confidential sale of his invention, his demonstration of its use to a private group, or a third party's unrestricted but private use of the invention will no longer constitute prior art. Only the sale or offer for sale of the invention to the relevant public or its use in a way that makes it publicly accessible will constitute prior art.

See 157 Cong. Rec. S5320 (daily ed. September 6, 2011). Conclusive resolution of this issue may become the task of the judiciary or the subject of further legislation.

[46] W.L. Gore & Associates v. Garlock, Inc., 721 F.2d 1540 (Fed. Cir. 1983).

[47] 149 F.3d 1368 (Fed. Cir. 1998).

[48] As earlier codified at 35 U.S.C. §273, the prior commercial user defense is subject to a number of additional qualifications. First, the defendant must have reduced the infringing subject matter to practice at least one year before the effective filing date of the application. Second, the defendant must have commercially used the infringing subject matter prior to the effective filing date of the patent. Finally, any reduction to practice or use must have been made in good faith, without derivation from the patentee or persons in privity with the patentee.

[49] 35 U.S.C. §273(b)(6)

[50] P.L. 112-29 at §5.

[51] 35 U.S.C. §111.

[52] P.L. 112-29 at §4.

[53] 35 U.S.C. §284.

[54] In re Seagate Technology, 497 F.3d 1360 (Fed. Cir. 2007) (en banc).

[55] See Beatrice Foods Co. v. New England Printing & Lithographing Co., 923 F.2d 1576, 1578 (Fed. Cir. 1991).

[56] See, e.g., Jon E. Wright, "Willful Patent Infringement and Enhanced Damages—Evolution and Analysis," 10 George Mason Law Review (2001), 97.

[57] Seagate Technologies, supra.

[58] Ibid.

[59] See, e.g., Fromson v. Western Litho Plate & Supply Co., 853 F.2d 1568, 1572 (Fed. Cir. 1988).

[60] 383 F.3d 1337 (Fed. Cir. 2004).

[61] Ibid., at 1341.

[62] P.L. 112-29 at §17.

[63] P.L. 112-29 at §6(a).

[64] P.L. 112-29 at §6(d).

[65] P.L. 112-29 at §12.

[66] P.L. 112-29 at §18.

[67] P.L. 112-29 at §6(a).

[68] P.L. 112-29 at §6(d).

[69] The American Inventors Protection Act of 1999, P.L. 106-113, was part of the Intellectual Property and Communications Omnibus Reform Act of 1999, attached by reference to the Consolidated Appropriations Act for Fiscal Year 2000. President Clinton signed this bill on November 29, 1999.

[70] Notably, the proposed restriction of inter partes review to patents and printed publications limits the grounds on which a patent challenger may request such a review. Once a patent is subject to inter partes review, the USPTO may potentially consider other pertinent patentability issues, such as claim definiteness.

[71] P.L. 112-29 at §12.

[72] 35 U.S.C. §122(a) (stating the general rule that "applications for patents shall be kept in confidence by the Patent and Trademark Office and no information concerning the same given without authority of the applicant....").

[73] Glaverbel Societe Anonyme v. Northlake Mktg. & Supply Inc., 45 F.3d 1550 (Fed. Cir. 1995).

[74] Therasense, Inc. v. Becton, Dickinson and Co., 649 F.3d 1276 (Fed. Cir. 2011).

[75] P.L. 112-29 at §18.

[76] 35 U.S.C. §301.

[77] P.L. 112-29 at §6(g)

[78] 37 C.F.R. §1.291.
[79] 35 U.S.C. §122(c).
[80] 37 C.F.R. §1.99.
[81] U.S. Dept. of Commerce, U.S. Patent & Trademark Off., Manual of Patent Examining Procedure §1134.01 (8th ed. July 2008).
[82] P.L. 112-29 at §9.
[83] 35 U.S.C. §2(b)(2). It should be appreciated that "Congress has not vested the [USPTO] with any general substantive rulemaking power...." Cybor Corp. v. FAS Techs, Inc., 138 F.3d 1448, 1479 (Fed. Cir. 1998) (en banc) (Newman, J., additional views).
[84] P.L. 112-29 at §10.
[85] P.L. 112-29 at §11.
[86] P.L. 112-29 at §22.
[87] P.L. 112-29 at §10(g)
[88] See CRS Report RL34221, Patents on Tax Strategies: Issues in Intellectual Property and Innovation, by John R. Thomas.
[89] P.L. 112-29 at §14.
[90] 35 U.S.C. §112.
[91] See, e.g., Chemcast Corp. v. Arco Industries Corp. 913 F.2d 923 (Fed. Cir. 1990).
[92] P.L. 112-29 at §15.
[93] Jerry R. Selinger, "In Defense of "Best Mode": Preserving the Benefit of the Bargain for the Public, 43 Catholic University Law Review (1994), 1099 ("Failure to comply with best mode ... is not something an examiner normally can evaluate when reviewing the application....").
[94] P.L. 112-29 at §19.
[95] Ibid., at §19(d).
[96] See CRS Report R41114, The Hatch-Waxman Act: Over a Quarter Century Later, by Wendy H. Schacht and John R. Thomas.
[97] 35 U.S.C. §1(b).
[98] P.L. 112-29 at §23.
[99] P.L. 112-29 at §24.
[100] See USPTO, Director's Forum: David Kappos' Public Blog, "Progress Report on Satellite Office Openings" (September 12, 2012) (available at http://www.uspto.gov /blog/director/entry/progress_report_on_satellite_office).
[101] P.L. 112-29 at §28.
[102] P.L. 112-29 at §25.
[103] See Commissioner of Patents and Trademarks, Policy Statement on Patentability of Animals, 1077 Off. Gaz. Pat. Office 24 (April 7, 1987).
[104] P.L. 112-29 at §33.
[105] 35 U.S.C. §156(d)(1).
[106] P.L. 112-29 at §37.
[107] See, e.g., Elizabeth M. Bailey et al., "Making Sense of 'Apportionment' in Patent Damages," 12 Columbia Science and Technology Law Review 255 (2011) (noting these concerns).
[108] See, e.g., Martha K. Gooding & William C. Rooklidge, "The Real Problem with Patent Infringement Damages," 91 Journal of the Patent and Trademark Office Society 484 (2009).
[109] 580 F.3d 1301 (Fed. Cir. 2009).
[110] See, e.g., Brad Smith, "In a Competitive Economy, The Country's Prosperity Depends More Than Ever on a Healthy Patent System," Inside Counsel 8 (May 1, 2010).
[111] 35 U.S.C. §122(b).

[112] See CRS Report RS20906, U.S. Patent and Trademark Office Appropriations Process: A Brief Explanation, by Wendy H. Schacht.

In: The Patent System
Editor: Deanna Hoffman

ISBN: 978-1-63482-267-1

Chapter 2

COMPULSORY LICENSING OF PATENTED INVENTIONS*

John R. Thomas

SUMMARY

The term "compulsory license" refers to the grant of permission for an enterprise seeking to use another's intellectual property without the consent of its proprietor. The grant of a compulsory patent license typically requires the sanction of a governmental entity and provides for compensation to the patent owner. Compulsory licenses in the patent system most often relate to pharmaceuticals and other inventions pertaining to public health, but they potentially apply to any patented invention.

U.S. law allows for the issuance of compulsory licenses in a number of circumstances, and also allows for circumstances that are arguably akin to a compulsory license. The Atomic Energy Act, Clean Air Act, and Plant Variety Protection Act provide for compulsory licensing, although these provisions have been used infrequently at best. The Bayh-Dole Act offers the federal government "march-in rights," although these have not been invoked in the three decades since that legislation has been enacted. 28 U.S.C. Section 1498 provides the U.S. government with broad ability to use inventions patented by others. Compulsory licenses have also been

* This is an edited, reformatted and augmented version of a Congressional Research Service publication R43266, prepared for Members and Committees of Congress, dated January 14, 2014.

awarded as a remedy for antitrust violations. Finally, a court may decline to award an injunction in favor of a prevailing patent owner during infringement litigation, an outcome that some observers believe is akin to the grant of a compulsory license.

A number of international agreements to which the United States and its trading partners are signatories, including the Paris Convention for the Protection of Industrial Property, World Trade Organization agreements, and certain free trade agreements, address compulsory licensing. In contrast to the United States, the patent statutes of many other nations include general provisions that allow for the award of compulsory licenses under specified conditions. A number of U.S. trading partners, including Brazil, South Africa, and Thailand, have invoked these provisions. The March 9, 2012, decision of the Indian government to grant a compulsory license on the chemotherapy drug sorafenib has attracted controversy.

Some commentators have expressed concern that compulsory licenses substantially diminish incentives for firms to conduct research and development. Others support the grant of such licenses under certain conditions, noting that many patent-granting states suffer from poverty, dire health needs, and a lack of access to patented technologies.

Congress has previously monitored the issuance of compulsory patent licenses by U.S. trading partners and may wish to continue to do so. Legislation dating from the 109th Congress would have allowed the Secretary of Health and Human Services to declare a compulsory license on a patented invention that was needed to address a public health emergency. This legislation was not enacted and has not been reintroduced.

INTRODUCTION

Congressional interest in the patent system has been demonstrated by the recent enactment of the Leahy-Smith America Invents Act (AIA),[1] arguably the most significant amendments to the patent laws since 1952.[2] Subsequent to the enactment of the AIA, Members of Congress have expressed criticism with respect to the grant of compulsory licenses on patented inventions by the trading partners of the United States.[3] Compulsory patent licenses have in fact been a longstanding source of tension between the United States and other nations.[4] However, U.S. law also provides for compulsory licensing of patented inventions under certain circumstances.[5]

The term "compulsory license" refers to the grant of permission for an enterprise seeking to use another's intellectual property to do so without the consent of its proprietor.[6] The grant of a compulsory patent license typically requires the sanction of a governmental entity and provides for compensation to the patent owner. In the patent system, compulsory licenses most often relate to pharmaceuticals and other inventions pertaining to public health, but they potentially apply to information technologies, manufacturing methods, and any other sort of patented invention.

For some observers, compulsory patent licenses present an unwise derogation from the exclusive rights awarded to patent owners. In their view, the routine grant of compulsory licenses will diminish incentives for innovation.[7] On the other hand, other observers believe that compulsory licenses may serve important national interests such as public health and technology transfer.[8]

This report provides an overview of compulsory licenses on patented inventions. It begins with a brief introduction of the patent system and the concept of compulsory patent licenses, including limitations imposed upon World Trade Organization members by the Agreement on Trade-Related Aspects of Intellectual Property Rights (the "TRIPS" Agreement).[9] The report next reviews the availability of compulsory licenses under U.S. law. The report next considers the practice of compulsory licensing on patented inventions abroad. The report closes with a discussion of the role of compulsory licenses in innovation policy and a review of possible congressional options.

PATENT FUNDAMENTALS

The patent system is grounded in Article I, Section 8, Clause 8 of the U.S. Constitution, which states that "The Congress Shall Have Power ... To promote the Progress of Science and useful Arts, by securing for limited Times to Authors and Inventors the exclusive Right to their respective Writings and Discoveries...." U.S. patent rights do not arise automatically. Inventors must prepare and submit applications to the U.S. Patent and Trademark Office (USPTO) if they wish to obtain patent protection.[10] USPTO officials known as examiners then assess whether the application merits the award of a patent.[11]

In deciding whether to approve a patent application, a USPTO examiner will consider whether the submitted application fully discloses and distinctly claims the invention.[12] In addition, the application must disclose the "best mode," or preferred way, that the applicant knows to practice the invention.[13]

The examiner will also determine whether the invention itself fulfills certain substantive standards set by the patent statute. To be patentable, an invention must consist of a process, machine, manufacture, or composition of matter that is useful, novel, and nonobvious. The requirement of usefulness, or utility, is satisfied if the invention is operable and provides a tangible benefit.[14] To be judged novel, the invention must not be fully anticipated by a prior patent, publication, or other state-of-the-art knowledge that is collectively termed the "prior art."[15] A nonobvious invention must not have been readily within the ordinary skills of a competent artisan at the time the invention was made.[16]

If the USPTO allows the patent to issue, the patent proprietor obtains the right to exclude others from making, using, selling, offering to sell, or importing into the United States the patented invention.[17] Those who engage in these acts without the permission of the patentee during the term of the patent can be held liable for infringement. Adjudicated infringers may be enjoined from further infringing acts.[18] The patent statute also provides for the award of damages "adequate to compensate for the infringement, but in no event less than a reasonable royalty for the use made of the invention by the infringer."[19]

The maximum term of patent protection is ordinarily set at 20 years from the date the application is filed.[20] At the end of that period, others may employ that invention without regard to the expired patent.

Patent rights are not self-enforcing. Patentees who wish to compel others to observe their rights must commence enforcement proceedings, which most commonly consist of litigation in the federal courts. Although issued patents enjoy a presumption of validity, accused infringers may assert that a patent is invalid or unenforceable on a number of grounds.[21] The U.S. Court of Appeals for the Federal Circuit (Federal Circuit) possesses national jurisdiction over most patent appeals from the district courts.[22] The U.S. Supreme Court enjoys discretionary authority to review cases decided by the Federal Circuit.[23]

INTRODUCTION TO COMPULSORY LICENSES

As noted, patents afford their owners the right to exclude others from practicing the patented invention.[24] Patent owners may decline to enforce their exclusionary rights and allow another entity to use their proprietary technology, however. This permission is typically granted in exchange for the payment of a royalty or other consideration. This private contractual arrangement is termed a "license."[25]

In addition to a voluntary license, patents may be subject to a compulsory license. Although no universally accepted definition exists, the term "compulsory license" implies that anyone who meets certain statutory criteria may use the patented invention. The permission of the patent owner is not required. Depending upon particular national laws, the grounds for government award of a compulsory license may include:

- Circumstances of national emergency or extreme urgency.
- Where the invention serves vital public health needs.
- A strong societal interest has arisen in access to the patented invention.
- The patent owner has failed to practice the patented invention in the jurisdiction that granted the patent within a reasonable period of time.
- The patent owner has abused its economic power in such a manner as to violate the antitrust laws.
- In circumstances where multiple patents held by different owners cover a particular technology. For example, combination therapies—such as triple antiretroviral drugs—may be subject to more than one patent. In such cases, if one patent owner refuses to license, then the technology may not be marketed absent a compulsory licensing.[26]

These statutes typically require an interested party formally to request the compulsory license from a foreign government. Competent authorities then decide whether to grant the license as well as the terms of any granted license. While some accounts suggest that formal compulsory licenses are awarded infrequently, the mere existence of a compulsory licensing statute may do much to encourage bargaining between a patentee and an interested manufacturer, on terms favorable to the manufacturer.[27]

Two notable multilateral international agreements address compulsory patent licenses. The first, the Convention of Paris for the Protection of Industrial Property,[28] has been joined by 175 countries including the United States.[29] The Paris Convention states that its member states "have the right to take legislative measures providing for the grant of compulsory licenses to prevent the abuses which might result from the exercise of the exclusive rights conferred by the patent, for example, failure to work."[30] Paris Convention member states have agreed that a compulsory license "may not be applied for on the ground of failure to work or insufficient working before the expiration of a period of four years from the date of filing of the patent application or three years from the date of the grant of the patent, whichever period expires last; it shall be refused if the patentee justifies his inaction by legitimate reasons."[31]

The other significant multilateral agreement that speaks to compulsory patent licensing, a component of the international agreements forming the World Trade Organization (WTO), is the Agreement on Trade-Related Aspects of Intellectual Property Rights.[32] The so-called "TRIPS Agreement" places further limitations upon the ability of WTO member states to award compulsory licenses for the use of another's patented invention. Among the most detailed provisions of the TRIPS Agreement, Article 31 imposes in part the following restrictions upon the issuance of compulsory licenses:

- Each application for a compulsory license must be considered on its individual merits.
- The proposed user must have made efforts to obtain authorization from the patent owner on reasonable commercial terms and conditions and such efforts have not been successful within a reasonable period of time. However, this requirement may be waived in the case of national emergency or other circumstances of extreme urgency.
- The scope and duration of the compulsory license is limited to the purpose for which it was authorized.
- The compulsory license must be nonexclusive—that is to say, the patent owner and possibly other licensed parties may also practice the patented invention.
- Any such use shall be authorized predominantly for the supply of the domestic market of the Member authorizing such use.
- The compulsory license must be revocable if and when its motivating circumstances cease to exist and are unlikely to recur.
- The patent owner must be paid adequate remuneration in the circumstances of each case, taking into account the economic value of the authorization.
- The legal validity of any decision relating to the authorization of such use shall be subject to judicial or other independent review.

Article 31(k) of the TRIPS Agreement waives some of these requirements when use of a patented invention "is permitted to remedy a practice determined after judicial or administrative practice to be anti-competitive." In addition, Article 31(l) allows for a compulsory license to issue to allow holders of improvement patents to make use of dominant patents that would otherwise bar the commercialization of an important technical advance.[33]

In November 2001, WTO signatories adopted the Doha Declaration on the TRIPS Agreement and Public Health.[34] The Doha Declaration stated that the TRIPS Agreement "can and should be interpreted and implemented in a manner supportive of WTO Members' right to protect public health and, in particular, to promote access to medicines for all." The Doha Declaration granted broad discretion with regard to compulsory licensing, asserting that WTO signatories have "the right to grant compulsory licences [sic] and the freedom to determine the grounds upon which such licences [sic] can be granted." In addition, WTO signatories proposed an amendment to the TRIPS Agreement in the form of Article 31bis. That provision allows WTO member states with limited or no manufacturing capacity to declare a compulsory license to import generic drugs from other countries.[35]

The conditions for compulsory licensing within the TRIPS Agreement involve a number of ambiguities. Such terms as "national emergency" or "circumstance of extreme urgency" are not further defined. It is arguably not clear what exactly is meant by the requirement that a compulsory license be granted primarily for the supply of the domestic market. Nor is there any precise definition of what level of "adequate remuneration" to the patent holder suffices. The application of these limitations may not be further understood until a competent tribunal is called upon to interpret them, an event that has yet to occur.[36]

In addition to the TRIPS Agreement and Paris Convention, the United States has entered into a number of free trade agreements that also address compulsory patent licenses. These agreements require their signatories to grant compulsory patent licenses on more restrictive terms than permitted by the TRIPS Agreement or Paris Convention. For example, the Free Trade Agreement between the United States and Australia[37] provides:

> A Party shall not permit the use of the subject matter of a patent without the authorisation of the right holder except in the following circumstances:
>
> (a) to remedy a practice determined after judicial or administrative process to be anticompetitive under the Party's laws relating to prevention of anti-competitive practices; or
>
> (b) in cases of public non-commercial use, or of national emergency, or other circumstances of extreme urgency, provided that:

(i) the Party shall limit such use to use by the government or third persons authorised by the government;

(ii) the Party shall ensure that the patent owner is provided with reasonable compensation for such use; and

(iii) the Party may not require the patent owner to provide undisclosed information or technical know-how related to a patented invention that has been authorised for use in accordance with this paragraph.[38]

To the extent that compliance with treaties is desired, member states of the Paris Convention, TRIPS Agreement, and other pertinent international agreements may need to take these provisions into account when addressing compulsory licensing.

COMPULSORY LICENSES UNDER U.S. LAW

In contrast to the patent statutes of many nations, the U.S. patent code does not include a general compulsory licensing provision. However, other domestic laws include provisions that allow for the compulsory licensing of patented inventions. In addition, circumstances that are arguably akin to a compulsory license may occur through antitrust enforcement, judicial determinations in patent infringement litigation, and activities of the federal government.

Specialized Statutes

A modest number of additional compulsory licenses exist with respect to U.S. patents, each pertaining to specialized subject matter.[39] For example, the Atomic Energy Act allows for compulsory licenses "if the invention or discovery covered by the patent is of primary importance in the production or utilization of special nuclear material or atomic energy."[40] The Clean Air Act contains a similar provision relating to devices for reducing air pollution.[41] Finally, the Plant Variety Protection Act provides for the compulsory licensing of seed-bearing plants that are protected by plant variety certificates, a patent-like instrument granted by the Department of Agriculture.[42]

Research completed in connection with this report has failed to discover even a single instance where any of these compulsory licenses has actually been invoked. Plainly, none of these provisions have been frequently employed in the past.[43] Some commentators speculate that the threat of a compulsory license usually induces the grant of contractual licenses on reasonable terms. As a result, there is no need for the government to invoke a compulsory license formally.[44]

Antitrust Enforcement

Enforcement of the antitrust laws by government entities and private parties on occasion results in a patent owner either agreeing to license its patents to competitors or being compelled to do so.[45] Stated broadly, if an enterprise has been found to have acted in an anticompetitive manner in connection with its patents, then government or private enforcement authorities may call for the enterprise to license those patents to interested parties.[46] This step is arguably akin to the grant of a compulsory license.

The Bayh-Dole Act

The Bayh-Dole Act and accompanying regulations allow government contractors to obtain patents on inventions they made using federal funding.[47] However, the government retains a "march-in right" that allows the funding agency to grant additional licenses to other "reasonable applicants."[48] March-in rights are available only where the contractor

- has not taken effective steps to achieve practical application of the invention;
- has not reasonably satisfied health and safety needs;
- has not met requirements for public use specified by federal regulation; or
- has granted an exclusive right to use the patented invention to another without obtaining the promise that the invention will be manufactured substantially in the United States.[49]

The march-in right, which is arguably identical or similar to a compulsory license, has yet to be exercised.[50]

Judicial Denial of Injunction

An injunction consists of a court order preventing or commanding a particular action. Prior to 2006, courts would virtually always enjoin an adjudicated infringer from future practice of the patented invention. This rule changed following the issuance of the Supreme Court decision in *eBay Inc. v. MercExchange, L.L.C.*[51] There the Court unanimously held that an injunction should not automatically issue based on a finding of patent infringement. Under the *eBay* ruling, courts must weigh equitable factors traditionally used to determine if an injunction should issue, including whether the patent proprietor suffered an irreparable injury; the award of damages would be inadequate to compensate for that injury; that considering the balance of hardships between the patent owner and infringer, an injunction is warranted; and that the public interest would not be disserved by a permanent injunction.[52]

Following the *eBay* decision, courts most often award an injunction to the prevailing patentee.[53] They have also declined to do so, however, particularly where the patent owner does not commercialize the claimed invention, where the patented invention forms a small component of a larger product, and where the patent owner had liberally licensed its patented invention to others.[54] In such cases the adjudicated infringer may continue to practice the patented invention but usually must pay a royalty to the patent proprietor until the term of the patent expires.[55]

Judicial unwillingness to enjoin an adjudicated infringer differs as a technical matter from the usual understanding of a compulsory license. Compulsory licenses are generally available to any entity that meets the statutory requirements, in contrast to the specific adjudicated infringer involved in a single litigation. As a result, some federal jurists prefer to use the term "ongoing royalty" to describe circumstances where courts have declined to award a permanent injunction but require the payment of royalties by the infringer during the term of the patent.[56] However, for some, the distinction between a compulsory license and an "ongoing royalty" is one without a difference.[57]

Uses by the U.S. Government

The U.S. government possesses the power to take private property for public use. For example, the government may condemn a parcel of land in order to build a highway. This authority is ordinarily termed "eminent domain." This government right is not unlimited, however. In particular, in some circumstances the government must compensate the property owner for use of the property.[58]

These general principles are most frequently applied to real estate, but they potentially apply to intellectual property as well.[59] As a result, the U.S. government effectively enjoys the ability to declare a compulsory license that allows it to use a patented invention without obtaining the permission of the patentee. In turn, the federal government has consented to suit by private patent owners in order to obtain compensation.[60] Section 1498(a) of Title 28 of the U.S. Code provides in part:

> Whenever an invention described in and covered by a patent of the United States is used or manufactured by or for the United States without license of the owner thereof or lawful right to use or manufacture the same, the owner's remedy shall be by action against the United States in the United States Claims Court for the recovery of his reasonable and entire compensation for such use and manufacture.

Under Section 1498(a), all patent suits against the U.S. government are litigated in the U.S. Court of Federal Claims. That statute limits available remedies to "reasonable and entire compensation" to the patent owner. As a result, the government may not be enjoined from practicing a patented invention. The courts have also generally limited the damages that the government must pay to the patentee to the level of a "reasonable royalty." A "reasonable royalty" for purposes of patent infringement damages is "the amount that a person desiring to manufacture or use a patented article, as a business proposition, would be willing to pay as a royalty and yet be able to make or use the patented article, in the market at a reasonable profit."[61]

COMPULSORY LICENSES ABROAD

The patent statutes of many U.S. trading partners include general provisions that allow for the award of compulsory licenses under specified conditions.[62] These circumstances include public health needs, inadequacy of supply of the patented invention, failure to practice the patented invention within the jurisdiction, and other public interest rationales.[63] Reportedly, a number of jurisdictions have invoked these provisions since the advent of the TRIPS Agreement, including, among others, Cameroon,[64] Ecuador,[65] Egypt,[66] Eritrea,[67] Ghana,[68] Italy,[69] Kenya,[70] Malaysia,[71] Mozambique,[72] Zambia,[73] and Zimbabwe.[74] This paper reviews a number of notable incidents with respect to compulsory licenses on patented inventions, focusing on Brazil, India, South Africa, and Thailand.

Brazil

In response to its accession to the WTO, Brazil enacted a new industrial property law that in part addressed compulsory patent licenses.[75] The 1997 statute allowed the issuance of compulsory licenses for "non-exploitation of the object of the patent within the Brazilian territory for failure to manufacture or incomplete manufacture of the product...."[76] The United States initiated proceedings before the WTO asserting that the Brazilian law violated the TRIPS Agreement. In particular, the United States alleged that the Brazilian statute violated a TRIPS Agreement requirement that patents must be "enjoyable without discrimination as to ... whether patents are imported or locally produced."[77] Brazil and the United States ultimately agreed to a "mutually satisfactory situation" under which Brazil agreed to hold talks with the U.S. government prior to granting compulsory license on patents owned by U.S. companies.[78] The WTO proceedings were then terminated.

Under the 1997 statute, Brazil issued a compulsory license in 2007 for the AIDS drug efavirenz, which is sold by Merck & Co. under the trademark STOCRIN®.[79] Reportedly Merck lowered the price under which it sold efavirnz to the satisfaction of the Brazilian authorities following the issuance of the compulsory license, thereby rendering this action moot.[80] In addition, the Brazilian government has reportedly used the threat of issuing compulsory licensing to receive discounts on AIDS therapies.[81]

India

On March 9, 2012, the Controller of Patents issued what is reportedly India's first compulsory license.[82] The compulsory license relates to the chemotherapy drug sorafenib, sold by Bayer & Co. under the trademark NEXAVAR®. According to the Controller, Bayer failed to provide sufficient NEXAVAR® to meet public demand, did not sell NEXAVAR® at a reasonably affordable price, and did not manufacture NEXAVAR® in India. As a result, the Controller awarded a license to Natco Pharma Ltd., an Indian generic firm, to manufacture a generic version of NEXAVAR®. Under the Controller's decision, Natco was required to pay a royalty at the rate of 6% of net sales of the drug to Bayer.[83] The Intellectual Property Appellate Board of India upheld the Controller's decision on March 4, 2013, although it increased the royalty owed to Bayer from 6% to 7%.[84]

Following the grant of the NEXAVAR® compulsory license, Indian authorities are reportedly considering the grant of compulsory licenses for Genetech's breast cancer drug HERCPETIN®, BMS's breast cancer drug IXEMPRA®, and BMS's leukemia drug SPRYCEL®.[85]

South Africa

In 1997, the South African legislature passed a law to allow, among other measures, the compulsory licensing of patented pharmaceuticals. The South African Pharmaceutical Manufacturers' Association and numerous pharmaceutical companies subsequently commenced litigation, asserting that the law violated both the TRIPS Agreement and South Africa's own patent statute. South Africa agreed to redraft in keeping with the TRIPS Agreement and to consult with the pharmaceutical industry on the proposed amendment, while the pharmaceutical industry agreed to withdraw the lawsuit.[86] Domestically, the incident reportedly prompted the issuance of Executive Order 13,155 by President Clinton on May 10, 2000. That Order prohibits the United States "from taking action pursuant to section 301(b) of the Trade Act of 1974 with respect to any law or policy in beneficiary sub-Saharan African countries that promotes access to HIV/AIDS pharmaceuticals or medical technologies and that provides adequate and effective intellectual property protection consistent with the TRIPS Agreement."[87]

Although the South African government apparently did not invoke the contested provisions, it subsequently determined that providers of two patented HIV/AIDS medicines had committed antitrust violations. In particular, in 2003 the South African Competition Commission concluded that the providers had engaged in excessive pricing and denied competitors access to an essential facility. The Commission subsequently settled with the providers on terms that required these providers to license several competitors to sell the patented medications.[88]

Thailand

Thailand issued seven compulsory patent licenses from 2006 through 2008. The compulsory licenses concerned patents claiming:

- the AIDS drug efavirenz (sold by Merck & Co. under the trademark STOCRIN®);[89]
- the combination AIDS drug of lopinavir and ritonavir (sold by Abbott under the trademark KALETRA®);[90]
- the antiplatelet drug clopidegrel (sold by Bristol Myers under the trademark PLAVIX®);[91]
- the breast cancer medicine letrozole (sold by Novartis AG under the trademark FEMARA®);[92]
- the breast and lung cancer drug docetaxel (sold by Sanofi-Aventis under the trademark TAXOTERE®);[93]
- the lung, pancreatic, and ovarian cancer drug erlotinib (sold by Roche under the trademark Tarceva TARCEVA®);[94] and
- the cancer drug Imitinab (sold by Novartis AG as GLEEVEC®).[95]

The Thai compulsory licenses attracted controversy due to their relatively large number, Thailand's status as a middle-income country, and concerns that the Thai government had not complied with the TRIPS Agreement.[96] In addition, five of the compulsory licenses concerned drugs for treating cancer and heart diseases—chronic, noninfectious diseases that are common in developed countries.[97] However, public health advocates applauded the Thai government's willingness to address the needs of its citizens.[98]

Issues and Observations

Observers who have supported the ability of patent-granting states to issue compulsory licenses have pointed out that the rules established under the TRIPS Agreement are quite liberal. Compulsory licenses are not limited to patents relating to contagious diseases; indeed, they are not limited to health emergencies at all. Under the TRIPS Agreement, any patent may potentially be subject to a compulsory license.[99] They also assert that the United States allows compulsory licenses to issue with respect to patents through a number of mechanisms.[100]

Still others observe that many least-developed and developing nations suffer from severe public health problems. These jurisdictions also may have limited ability to pay for patented medications.[101] Further, in the view of some commentators, because many of these nations offer small markets, their use of compulsory licenses is likely to have a negligible impact on innovation.[102]

On the other hand, some commentators believe that the grant of compulsory licenses diminishes incentives for enterprises to undertake research and development.[103] In their view, the pharmaceutical industry is less likely to endeavor to develop new drugs if they can expect that their patents will be subject to compulsory licenses, thereby causing the industry to lose its expected earnings.[104] To the extent that the U.S. firms are subject to these measures, the issuance of compulsory licenses may also negatively impact the U.S. economy.[105]

Commentators have also observed that although most compulsory licenses have been issued by developing and least-developed nations, these jurisdictions might have the most to lose by doing so. Pharmaceutical firms might devote fewer resources towards developing cures for diseases, such as malaria and tuberculosis, which primarily plague the developing world. Instead, a rational actor would allocate resources towards medicines that are likely to have a successful commercial market in developed countries.[106] In addition, the issuance of compulsory licenses may discourage foreign direct investment in that jurisdiction.[107]

Should Congress consider current circumstances with respect to compulsory licenses to be appropriate, then no action need be taken. Alternatively, Congress may wish to review whether domestic legislation providing for compulsory patent licenses is appropriate. The most recent bill relating to compulsory licensing, the Public Health Emergency Medicines Act in the 109th Congress, would have created an additional compulsory license in the patent law. This bill, H.R. 4131, would have allowed the government to use the patented invention without the patent owner's permission if the Secretary of Health and Human Services determined that the invention is needed to address a public health emergency. Under the bill, the Secretary of Health and Human Services would have determined compensation for government use of the patented invention. In determining the reasonableness of remuneration for use of a patent, the Secretary of Health and Human Services may consider—

1) evidence of the risks and costs associated with the invention claimed in the patent and the commercial development of products that use the invention;
2) evidence of the efficacy and innovative nature and importance to the public health of the invention or products using that invention;
3) the degree to which the invention benefitted from publicly funded research;
4) the need for adequate incentives for the creation and commercialization of new inventions;
5) the interests of the public as patients and payers for health care services;
6) the public health benefits of expanded access to the invention;
7) the benefits of making the invention available to working families and retired persons;
8) the need to correct anti-competitive practices; and
9) other public interest considerations.108

This legislation was not enacted.

Congress may also wish to continue to monitor the activity of U.S. trade partners with respect to compulsory patent licenses. For example, on June 18, 2013, 171 Members of Congress wrote to President Obama expressing concern over India's "intellectual property (IP) climate." The letter in part observed:

> [T]he Indian Government issued its first compulsory license (CL) on a stage three liver and kidney cancer drug. It has been reported that additional drugs may be subject to CLs imminently and that the decisions related to these CLs are being improperly driven by an interest in growing the pharmaceutical market in India. These actions by the Indian Government greatly concern us because innovation and the protection of intellectual property are significant driving engines of the U.S. economy.[109]

The letter urged the President "to make sure these issues are raised at the highest levels of the Indian government."

Compulsory licenses for patented inventions highlight the tension between two competing aspirations of the patent system: Encouraging the labors that lead to innovation, on one hand, and placing the fruits of those labors before the public, on the other. As different patent-granting states possess distinct perceived interests and values with respect to innovation, proprietary rights, and public health and other social needs, conflicts among these jurisdictions have occurred in the post-WTO era. Assessing the role of compulsory licenses within the patent system of the United States and our trading partners remains a matter for congressional judgment.

End Notes

[1] P.L. 112-29 (September 16, 2011).

[2] P.L. 82-593 (July 19, 1952).

[3] See Hearing Before the House Committee on the Judiciary, Subcommittee on Intellectual Property, Competition and the Internet, on "International IP Enforcement: Protecting Patents, Trade Secrets and Market Access" (June 27, 2012), 16 (available at http://judiciary.house.gov/hearings/printers/112th/112-119_74817.PDF).

[4] See Christopher Gibson, "A Look at the Compulsory License in Investment Arbitration: The Case of Indirect Expropriation," 25 American University International Law Review (2010), 357.

[5] See Johanna Jacob, "Should Our Genes Be Part of the Patent Bargain? Maximizing Access to Medical Diagnostic Advances While Ensuring Research Remains Profitable," 28 Santa Clara Computer & High Technology Law Journal (2012), 403.

[6] See Jarrod Tudor, "Compulsory Licensing in the European Union," 4 George Mason Journal of Comparative Law (2013), 222.

[7] See Jon Matthews, "Renewing Healthy Competition: Compulsory Licenses and Why Abuses of the TRIPS Article 31 Standards Are Most Dangerous to the United States Healthcare Industry," 4 Journal of Business, Entrepreneurship, and the Law (2010), 119.

[8] See, e.g., Chris Strobel, "Wind Power and Patent Law: How the Enforcement of Wind Technology Patents May Lead to Restricted Implementation in the US, and Necessary Solutions," 19 Journal of Environmental and Sustainability Law (Spring 2013).

[9] See Agreement on Trade-Related Aspects of Intellectual Property Rights, April 15, 1994, Annex 1C, 33 I.L.M. 1197 (1994).

[10] 35 U.S.C. §111.

[11] 35 U.S.C. §131.

[12] 35 U.S.C. §112.

[13] Ibid.

[14] 35 U.S.C. §101.

[15] 35 U.S.C. §102.

[16] 35 U.S.C. §103.

[17] 35 U.S.C. §271(a).

[18] 35 U.S.C. §283.

[19] 35 U.S.C. §284.

[20] 35 U.S.C. §154(a)(2). Although patent term is based upon the filing date, the patentee gains no enforceable legal rights until the USPTO allows the application to issue as a granted patent.

A number of Patent Act provisions may modify the basic 20-year term, including examination delays at the USPTO and delays in obtaining marketing approval for the patented invention from other federal agencies.

[21] 35 U.S.C. §282.

[22] 28 U.S.C. §1295(a)(1).

[23] 28 U.S.C. §1254(1).

[24] 35 U.S.C. §271.

[25] See, e.g., Quanta Computer, Inc. v. LG Electronics, Inc., 553 U.S. 617 (2008).

[26] See, e.g., Katharine W. Sands, "Prescription Drugs: India Values Their Compulsory Licensing Provision—Should the United States Follow in India's Footsteps?," 29 Houston International Law Journal (2006), 191.

[27] See Robert P. Merges, "Intellectual Property Rights and the Bargaining Breakdown: The Case of Blocking Patents," 62 TennesSee Law Review (1994), 75.

[28] 13 I.S.T. 25 (1962) ("Paris Convention").

[29] The list of signatories is available at http://www.wipo.int.

[30] Paris Convention, Art. 5(A)(2). The phrase "failure to work" indicates that the patent proprietor has not practiced the patented invention in that jurisdiction.

[31] Ibid. Art. 5(A)(4).

[32] Agreement on Trade-Related Aspects of Intellectual Property Rights, April 15, 1994, Annex 1C, 33 I.L.M. 1197 (1994).

[33] See Jerome H. Reichman, "Intellectual Property in the Twenty-First Century: Will the Developing Countries Lead or Follow?," 46 Houston Law Review (2009), 1115.

[34] See World Trade Organization, Ministerial Declaration of 14 November 2001, WT/MIN(01)/DEC/1,41.I.L.M. 746.

[35] See Dina Halajian, "Inadequacy of TRIPS and the Compulsory License: Why Broad Compulsory Licensing Is Not a Viable Solution to the Access to Medicine Problem," 38 Brooklyn Journal of International Law (2013), 1191.

[36] See Daniel R. Cahoy, "Breaking Patents," 32 Michigan Journal of International Law (2011), 461.

[37] United States-Australia Free Trade Agreement, 118 Stat. 919 (May 18, 2004).

[38] Ibid. at Chapter 17.9, Paragraph 7.

[39] Dawson Chemical Co. v. Rohm and Haas Co., 448 U.S. 176 n.21 (1980).

[40] 42 U.S.C. §2183 (2006).

[41] 42 U.S.C. §7608 (2006).

[42] 7 U.S.C. §2404 (2006).

[43] See Kenneth J. Nunnenkamp, "Compulsory Licensing of Critical Patents Under CERCLA?," 9 Journal of Natural Resources and Environmental Law (1993-94), 397, 406 (noting that "there Seems to have been no attempts to actually use the compulsory licensing provision" of the Clean Air Act).

[44] Stephen Pericles Ladas, Patents,Trademarks and Related Rights: National and International Protection (Cambridge, Mass., Harvard University Press 1975), 427.

[45] See Colleen Chien, "Cheap Drugs at What Price to Innovation: Does the Compulsory Licensing of Pharmaceuticals Hurt Innovation?," 18 Berkeley Technology Law Journal (2003), 853.

[46] See, e.g., Untied States v. 3D Systems Corp., 2001 WL 964343 (D.D.C. 2001).

[47] See CRS Report RL32076, The Bayh-Dole Act: Selected Issues in Patent Policy and the Commercialization of Technology, by Wendy H. Schacht.

[48] 35 U.S.C. §203(a).

[49] Ibid.

[50] See Nida Shakir, "The National Institutes of Health, Patents, and the Public Interest: An Expanded Rationale of Justice Breyer's Dissent in Stanford v. Roche," 17 Marquette Intellectual Property Law Review (Winter 2013), 143

[51] 547 U.S. 388 (2006).

[52] See Mark P. Gergen et al., "The Supreme Court's Accidental Revolution: The Test for Permanent Injunctions," 112 Columbia Law Review (2012), 203.

[53] See University of Houston Law Center, Patstats: U.S. Patent Litigation Statistics (June 19, 2013) (available at http://www.patstats.org/Patstats3.html).

[54] Ronald J. Schultz & Patrick M. Arenz, "Non-Practicing Entities and Permanent Injunctions Post-eBay," 12 Sedona Conference Journal (2011), 203.

[55] See ActiveVideo Networks, Inc. v. Verizon Communications, Inc., 694 F.3d 1312 (Fed. Cir. 2012).

[56] See Paice LLC v. Toyota Motor Corp., 504 F.3d 1293, 1313 n.13 (Fed. Cir. 2007).

[57] See Andrew C. Mace, "TRIPS, eBay, and Denials of Injunctive Relief: Is Article 31 Compliance Everything?," 10 Columbia Science & Technology Law Review (2009), 232.

[58] See CRS Report RS20741, The Constitutional Law of Property Rights "Takings": An Introduction, by Robert Meltz.

[59] Thomas F. Cotter, "Do Federal Uses of Intellectual Property Implicate the Fifth Amendment?," 50 Florida Law Review (1998), 529.

[60] See Lionel Marks Lavenue, "Patent Infringement Against the United States and Government Contractors Under 28 U.S.C. §1498(a) in the United States Court of Federal Claims," 2 Journal of Intellectual Property Law (1995), 389.

[61] Wright v. United States, 53 Fed. Cl. 466 (2002).

[62] See Cole M. Fauver, "Compulsory Patent Licensing in the United States: An Idea Whose Time Has Come," 8 Northwestern Journal of International Law and Business (1988), 666.

[63] See Christopher Gibson, "A Look at the Compulsory License in Investment Arbitration: The Case of Indirect Expropriation," 25 American University International Law Review (2010), 357.

[64] See Vera Zolotaryova, "Are We There Yet? Taking 'TRIPS' to Brazil and Expanding Access to HIV/AIDS Medication," 33 Brooklyn Journal of International Law (2008), 1099.

[65] See Donald Harris, "TRIPS After Fifteen Years: Success or Failure, As Measured by Compulsory Licensing," 18 Journal of Intellectual Property Law (2011), 367.

[66] See Sean Baird, "Magic and Hope: Relaxing TRIPS-Plus Provisions to Promote Access to Affordable Pharmaceuticals," 33 Boston College Journal of Law & Social Justice (2013), 107.

[67] See Harris, supra.

[68] Ibid.

[69] See Jarrod Tudor, "Compulsory Licensing in the European Union," 4 George Mason Journal of International Commercial Law (2013), 222.

[70] See Harris, supra.

[71] See Umar R. Bakhsh, "The Plumpy'Nut Predicament: Is Compulsory Licensing a Solution?", 11 Chicago-Kent Journal of Intellectual Property (2012), 238.

[72] See Zolotaryova, supra.

[73] Ibid.

[74] See Harris, supra.

[75] See Naomi A. Bass, "Implication of the TRIPS Agreement for Developing Countries: Pharmaceutical Patent Laws in Brazil and South Africa in the 21st Century," 34 George Washington International Law Review (2002), 191.

[76] Ibid. at Art. 68 (1)(I).

[77] TRIPS Agreement, Art. 27(1).

[78] Brazil—Measures Affecting Patent Protection, WT/DS199/4 (July 19, 2001).

[79] See Mariana Moto Prado, "The Debatable Role of Courts in Brazil's Health Care System: Does Litigation Harm or Help?," 41 Journal of Law, Medicine & Ethics (Spring 2013), 124.

[80] See Riadh Quadir, "Patent Stalemate? The WTO's Essential Medicines Impasse Between Pharmas and Least Developed Countries," 61 Rutgers Law Review (2009), 437.

[81] See Zita Lazzarini, "Making Access to Pharmaceuticals A Reality: Legal Options Under TRIPS and the Case of Brazil," 6 Yale Human Rights and Development Law Journal (2003), 103.

[82] See Naval Satarawala Chopra & Dinoo Muthappa, "The Curious Case of Compulsory Licensing in India," 8 Competition Law International (August 2012), no. 2 at 34.

[83] Natco Pharma Limited v Bayer Corporation, Compulsory Licence Application No 1/2011 (March 9, 2012) (available at http://patentdocs.typepad.com/files/compulsory-license-application.pdf).

[84] O.R.A. no. 35/PT/2012.

[85] See Tracy Staton, "India to Hit Roche, BMS with Compulsory License on 3 Cancer Drugs," FiercePharma (January 13, 2013) (available at http://www.fiercepharma.com/story/india-hit-roche-bms-compulsory-licenses-3-cancer-drugs/ 2013-01-13).

[86] See Erika George, "The Human Right to Health and HIV/AIDS: South Africa and South-South Cooperation to Reframe Global Intellectual Property Principles and Promote Access to Essential Medicines," 18 Indiana Journal of Global Legal Studies (2011), 167.

[87] 65 Fed. Reg. 30521, 30522.

[88] See Sarah Bosley, "Ruling Open the Door for Cut-Price HIV Drugs," The Guardian (October 17, 2003)

[89] Thawach Suntrajarn, Director General, Announcement of the Department of Disease Control, Ministry of Public Health, Thailand on the Public Use of Patent for Pharmaceutical Products (available at http://www.cptech.org/ip/health/c/thailand/thaicl4efavirenz.html).

[90] Thawach Suntrajarn, Director General, Decree of Department of Disease Control, Ministry of Public Heath, "Regarding Exploitation of Patent on Drugs and Medical Supplies by the Government on Combination Drug Between Lopinavir and Ritonavir" (January 29, 2007) (available at http://www.cptech.org/ip/health/c/thailand/thai-clkaletra_en.pdf).

[91] Prat Boonyawongvirot, Permanent Secretary, Ministry of Public Health, "Announcement Regarding Exploitation of Patents on Drugs and Medical Supplies for Clopidogrel" (January 25, 2007) (available at http://www.cptech.org/ip/health/c/thailand/thai-cl-clopidogrel_en.pdf).

[92] Ministry of Public Health and the National Health Security Office, "The 10 Burning Questions on the Government Use of Patents on the Four Anti-Cancer Drugs in Thailand" (February 2008) (available at http://www.moph.go.th/hot/ Second_white_paper_on_ the_ Thai_CL_%5BEN%5D.pdf).

[93] Ibid.

[94] Ibid.

[95] Ibid.

[96] Mingchanok Tejavanija, "A New Kind of Drug War: Thailand's Taking on the Pharmaceutical Industry to Improve Access to HIV/AIDS Drugs Through the Use of Compulsory Licensing," 28 Arizona Journal of International and Comparative Law (2011), 659.

[97] Nattapong Suwan-In, "Compulsory License, a Long Debate on TRIPS Agreement Interpretation: Discovering the Truth of Thailand's Imposition on Pharmaceutical Patents," 7 Asian Journal of WTO & International Health Law & Policy (2012), 225.

[98] Ibid.

[99] See Cynthia M. Ho, "Patent Breaking or Balancing?: Separating Strands of Fact from Fiction Under TRIPS," 34 North Carolina Journal of International Law and Commercial Regulation," 34 North Carolina Journal of International Law and Commercial Regulation (2009), 371.

[100] See James Love and Tim Hubbard, "Prizes for Innovation in New Medicines and Vaccines," 18 Annals of Health Law (Summer 2009), 155.

[101] See Rudolf V. Van Puymbroeck, "Basic Survival Needs and Access to Medicines—Coming to Grips with TRIPS: Conversion+Calculation," 38 Journal of Law, Medicine & Ethics (2010), 520.

[102] See Kristina M. Lybecker and Elisabeth Fowler, "Compulsory Licensing in Canada and Thailand: Comparing Regimes to Ensure Legitimate Use of the WTO Rules," 37 Journal of Law, Medicine & Ethics (2009), 222.

[103] See Richard A. Epstein and F. Scott Kieff, "Questioning the Frequency and Wisdom of Compulsory Licensing for Pharmaceutical Patents," 78 University of Chicago Law Review (2011), 71.

[104] See Samuel Mark Borowski, "Saving Tomorrow from Today: Preserving Innovation in the Face of Compulsory Licensing," 36 Florida State University Law Review (2009), 275.

[105] See Jamie Feldman, "Compulsory Licenses: The Dangers Behind Current Practice," 8 Journal of International Business Law (2009), 137.

[106] Stephanie Skees, "Thai-Ing Up the TRIPS Agreement: Are Compulsory Licenses the Answer to Thailand's AIDS Epidemic?," 19 Pace International Law Review (2007), 233.

[107] See Lawrence A. Kogan, "Commercial High Technology Innovations Face Uncertain Future Amid Emerging 'BRICS' Compulsory Licensing and Its Interoperability Frameworks," 13 San Diego International Law Journal (2011), 201.

[108] H.R. 4131, Section 2 (proposing to add a new §158 to the Patent Act). The bill had been previously introduced in the 109th Congress as H.R. 4102.

[109] The letter is available at http://paulsen.house.gov/uploads/India%20IP% 20Letter% 20Signed.pdf.

In: The Patent System
Editor: Deanna Hoffman
ISBN: 978-1-63482-267-1

Chapter 3

Gene Patents: A Brief Overview of Intellectual Property Issues*

John R. Thomas

Summary

In the past, the U.S. courts upheld gene patents that met the criteria of patentability defined by the Patent Act. However, the practice of awarding patents on genes came under scrutiny by some scientists, legal scholars, politicians, and other experts. In June 2013, the Supreme Court ruled in *Association for Molecular Pathology v. Myriad Genetics, Inc.* that genomic DNA was ineligible for patenting under 35 U.S.C. §101 due to the "product of nature" doctrine. However, the Court adopted the view that cDNA could be patented. The *Myriad* holding attempts to provide inventors and firms with incentives to conduct R&D while recognizing that patent proprietors might obtain too much control over medical practice and future research.

---

* This is an edited, reformatted and augmented version of a Congressional Research Service publication RS22516, prepared for Members and Committees of Congress, dated January 15, 2014.

Patents

The Patent Act of 1952, codified in Title 35 of the United States Code, defines current patent law. According to section 101, one who "invents or discovers any new and useful process, machine, manufacture, or any composition of matter, or any new and useful improvement thereof, may obtain a patent therefore, subject to the conditions and requirements of this title." To be patentable, an invention must be useful, novel, and nonobvious. The requirement of usefulness, or utility, is satisfied if the invention is operable and provides a tangible benefit. To be judged novel, the invention must not be fully anticipated by a prior patent, publication, or other knowledge within the public domain. A nonobvious invention must not have been readily within the ordinary skills of a competent artisan at the time the invention was made. The invention must be fully described. Once the United States Patent and Trademark Office (USPTO) issues a patent, the owner enjoys the right to exclude others from making, using, selling, offering to sell, or importing into the United States the patented invention. Generally, the term of a patent is 20 years from the date the application was filed. In the process of obtaining a patent, the information associated with the patent is published and made available to the public.

Gene Patents

In a June 2013 decision, the Supreme Court of the United States ruled in *Association for Molecular Pathology v. Myriad Genetics, Inc.*,[1] that genomic DNA was ineligible for patenting under 35 U.S.C. §101 because of the "product of nature" doctrine. Products of nature (preexisting substances found in the wild) may not be patented, *per se*. However, the courts have also determined that such a product of nature may be patentable if significant artificial changes are made. By purifying, isolating, or otherwise altering a naturally occurring product, an inventor may obtain a patent on the product in its altered form.[2]

Adopting the view that isolated and purified genomic DNA satisfied this exception to the "product of nature" doctrine, the USPTO issued over 50,000 patents relating at least in part to DNA.[3] However, some experts believed that the decision to patent human genes misconstrued the "product of nature" principle. In their view, the fact that scientists have isolated a gene is a "technicality" that did not allow genes to be patented.[4]

The Supreme Court decision in *Myriad* reflects this latter position. The litigation commenced on May 12, 2009, when the Association for Molecular Pathology and 19 other plaintiffs, including individual physicians, patients, and researchers, filed a lawsuit against the USPTO, Myriad Genetics, Inc., and the Directors of the University of Utah Research Foundation. The plaintiffs challenged several patents owned by Myriad that claim isolated human genes known as BRCA1 and BRCA2.[5] Certain alterations or mutations in these genes are associated with a predisposition to breast and ovarian cancers. Due to its intellectual property rights, Myriad was the sole commercial provider of genetic testing related to breast and ovarian cancer associated with the BRCA1 and BRCA2 genes. The plaintiffs asserted that Myriad's gene patent claims were invalid because, in their view, human genes are naturally occurring products that do not constitute patentable subject matter.

The U.S. District Court for the Southern District of New York sided with the plaintiffs and held that Myriad's gene patent claims were invalid under 35 U.S.C. §101.[6] Judge Sweet reasoned that Myriad's claimed isolated DNA was not "markedly different from native DNA as it exists in nature" and therefore could not be patented.[7] Following an appeal, the Federal Circuit reversed this holding.[8] The Court of Appeals reasoned that "isolated" DNA is not merely "purified" DNA—rather, it has been "manipulated chemically so as to produce a molecule that is markedly different from that which exists in the body."[9] Under this reasoning, human genes consist of patentable subject matter.

The Supreme Court subsequently agreed to hear the *Myriad* case but did not issue a ruling in the matter. Rather, on March 26, 2012, the Court vacated the judgment and remanded the matter back to the Federal Circuit with instructions to reconsider the appeal. The Federal Circuit responded by once again holding that both isolated DNA and cDNA were patent eligible.[10] The Supreme Court then granted *certiorari*.[11]

Justice Thomas, writing for the Court, initially observed that Myriad had neither created nor altered the generic information encoded in the BRCA1 and BRCA2 genes. Rather, Myriad had discovered the precise location and genetic sequence of those genes. According to Justice Thomas, then, "Myriad did not create anything. To be sure, it found an important and useful gene, but separating that gene from its surrounding genetic material is not an act of invention."[12] The Supreme Court also was unimpressed that Myriad claimed DNA that had been isolated from the human genome through the severing of chemical bonds, with a non-naturally occurring molecule as a result.

According to Justice Thomas, "Myriad's claims are simply not expressed in terms of chemical composition, nor do they rely in any way on the chemical changes that result from the isolation of a particular section of DNA."[13]

The Court took a more favorable view of cDNA, however. Observing that "cDNA retains the naturally occurring exons of DNA, but it is distinct from the DNA from which it was derived," Justice Thomas concluded that cDNA did not constitute a "product of nature" and therefore could be patented.

Justice Thomas also found it important to note what the *Myriad* opinion did not implicate. The case involved neither an innovative method of manipulating genes while searching for the BRCA1 and BRCA2 genes, the Court explained, nor new applications of knowledge about those genes. The Court also indicated that it had not considered the patentability of DNA in which the order of the naturally occurring nucleotides has been altered. Instead, the Court "merely [held] that genes and the information they encode are not patent eligible under §101 simply because they have been isolated from the surrounding genetic material."[14]

The opinion of Justice Thomas was joined in full by seven of his colleagues. Justice Scalia contributed a one-paragraph concurring opinion that joined the judgment of the Court and all of its opinion except those portions "going into fine details of molecular biology."[15] Justice Scalia found himself "unable to affirm those details on my own knowledge or even my own belief."[16] This shortcoming did not prevent him from concluding that isolated genomic DNA was identical to its natural state, however, while cDNA could be patented because it was a synthetic creation not found in nature.

Shortly after the Supreme Court issued its ruling, Myriad Genetics, Inc. and other plaintiffs commenced patent infringement litigation against certain genetic testing service providers.[17] Although the Supreme Court invalidated Myriad's claims on genomic DNA, Myriad asserted claims toward other genetic technologies. These claims recite in part, among other subject matter, a "method for detecting a germline alteration in a BRCA1 gene,"[18] an "isolated DNA coding for a BRCA1 polypeptide,"[19] a "method for screening germline of a human subject for an alteration of a BRCA1 gene,"[20] and a "pair of single-stranded DNA primers."[21] This litigation may provide further guidance as to the patentability of gene-related inventions in the wake of the Supreme Court's decision.

LEGAL ISSUES

The *Myriad* holding is expected to make it difficult for inventors to protect early, gene-related discoveries through the patent system. In particular, how the courts will apply the decision to other biologic products, including antisense DNA, microRNA, nucleic acids, proteins, and stem cells remains to be seen. However, the Supreme Court appears to approve of patent claims drawn to chemical modifications of naturally occurring substances, particularly if that modification endows the substance with a new property. For example, even slightly altered genes would appear to comprise patentable subject matter. As the USPTO explained in a memorandum released hours after the *Myriad* case issued:

> As of today, naturally occurring nucleic acids are not patent eligible merely because they have been isolated. Examiners should now reject product claims drawn solely to naturally occurring nucleic acids or fragments thereof, whether isolated or not, as being ineligible subject matter under 35 U.S.C. §101. Claims clearly limited to non-naturally-occurring nucleic acids, such as a cDNA or a nucleic acid in which the order of the naturally occurring nucleotides has been altered (e.g., a man-made variant sequence), remain eligible. Other claims, including method claims, that involve naturally occurring nucleic acids may give rise to eligibility issues and should be examined under the existing guidance ... [22]

Firms that employ cDNA to develop novel therapeutic proteins stand to benefit from the *Myriad* case. Still, one wonders if the Court neglected to recall its earlier holding in *Mayo v. Prometheus*[23] that that conventional or obvious pre-solution activity does not transform an unpatentable law of nature into a patent-eligible application of such law. cDNA is derived from DNA and is identical to DNA except that the non-coding regions have been removed—a choice dictated by natural laws and not the inventor. Further, the production of cDNA is reportedly well-understood and routine. Arguably, then, no scientific distinction pertinent to patent eligibility exists between genomic DNA and cDNA. Under *Myriad*, however, DNA is not patentable subject matter but cDNA may be patented.

Ethical Issues

Gene patents have been subject to a longstanding debate. Although the Supreme Court declared that genomic DNA may not be patented, it held that cDNA fulfills the requirements of 35 U.S.C. §101. In addition, the USPTO has issued other sorts of gene-related inventions, including those relating to genetic screening methods, polypeptides, DNA primers, and other technologies. As a result, the debate on gene patents potentially remains active. Some of its main contours are outlined below.

An often held belief is that gene patents permit outsiders ownership of another person's genetic makeup, often without their knowledge or consent.[24] This concern led to complaints that patients no longer control their own bodies and doctors are being constrained from testing for various diseases.[25] Professor Lori Andrews argues that patents hinder access to testing procedures because "gene-patent holders can control any use of 'their' gene; they can prevent a doctor from testing a patient's blood for a specific genetic mutation and can stop anyone from doing research to improve a genetic test or to develop a gene therapy based on that gene."[26] This perceived constraint on research and testing options is an issue to opponents of gene patents.[27] According to Dr. Debra Leonard, patents on "specific genetic information limits the medical use of the information and impedes or prevents widespread research on the disease, the traditional pathway by which medical knowledge is advanced and shared."[28]

However, other experts disagree. As noted by Dr. Jorge Goldstein and Attorney Elina Golod, the courts have consistently "taken the position that a person does not own any tissues or cells once they are outside the person's body."[29] Attorneys Lee Bendekgey and Dr. Diana Hamlet-Cox found no evidence of patients unable to utilize existing genetic tests because of patents. Instead, they maintain, it is a financial issue associated with the cost of health care and/or an issue of profits for the doctor or clinical geneticist wishing to administer tests patented by other inventors.[30] Similarly, Professor Iain Cockburn found "there is little quantitative evidence thus far of a negative impact of patents on scientific research activity.... "[31] From his perspective, the disclosure obligations of the patent system may better serve the objective of encouraging the diffusion of knowledge and raising social returns than the chief legal alternative, trade secret protection.[32]

ECONOMIC ISSUES

Actual experience and cited studies suggest that companies which do not control the results of their investments—either through ownership of patent title, exclusive license, or pricing decisions—tend to be less likely to engage in related R&D. Patents can provide an economic incentive for companies to pursue further development and commercialization. Studies indicate that research funding accounts for approximately one-quarter of the costs associated with bringing a new product to market. According to *The Economist*, "A dollar's worth of academic invention or discover requires upwards of $10,000 of private capital to bring [it] to market."[33] Patent ownership is seen as a way to encourage the additional, and often substantial investment necessary for new goods and services, particularly in the case of small business. In an academic setting, the possession of title to inventions is expected to provide motivation for the university to license the technology to the private sector for commercialization in anticipation of royalty payments.

While various analyses indicate that the value of patents differs across industries and between firms of different maturation levels within a sector,[34] the pharmaceutical industry perceives patents as critical to protecting innovation. Several studies over the years have demonstrated the important role patents play in the pharmaceutical sector. Of the 18 major manufacturing industries analyzed by Richard Levin and his colleagues, only drug companies rated product patents the most effective means of ensuring that firms can capture the profits associated with their innovations.[35] Later research by Professor Wesley Cohen *et.al* demonstrated that patents were considered the most effective method to protect inventions in the drug industry, particularly when biotechnology is included.[36] A recent paper by several professors at the Berkeley School of Law, University of California, found that there were "substantial differences between the health-related sectors (biotechnology and medical devices), in which patents are more commonly used and considered important, and the software and Internet fields, in which patents are reported to be less useful."[37] These studies reinforce earlier work by the late Professor Edwin Mansfield that indicated 65% of pharmaceutical inventions would not have been brought to market without patent protection in contrast to the 8% of innovations made in other industries.[38]

Patents may be particularly important in the pharmaceutical sector because of the relative ease of replicating the finished product. Imitation costs vary among industries. For example, while it is expensive, complicated, and time consuming to duplicate an airplane, it is relatively simple to chemically analyze a pill and reproduce it.[39] The degree to which industry perceives patents as effective has been characterized as "positively correlated with the increase in duplication costs and time associated with patents."[40] Other commentators note that patents are particularly important in this sector because of the relative ease of replicating the finished product. Costs associated with imitating a product "are extremely low relative to the innovator's costs for discovering and developing a new compound."[41] Early research in this area by Mansfield indicated that, in certain industries, patents significantly raise the costs incurred by nonpatent holders wishing to use the idea or invent around the patent—an estimated 40% in the pharmaceutical sector, 30% for major new chemical products, and 25% for typical chemical goods—and are thus viewed as significant. However, in other industries, patents have much smaller impact on the costs associated with imitation (e.g., in the 7%-15% range for electronics), and may be considered less successful in protecting resource investments.[42]

Opponents of gene patents argue that they restrain additional research because "there are no alternatives to a patented gene in diagnosis, treatment, and research,"[43] and owners require licensing fees.[44] However, despite what some experts claim to be a negative result of financial considerations in the biomedical research community,[45] others maintain that, at most, gene patents "prevent the doctors and clinical geneticists from performing these tests for profit, or in a way that competes with the patent holder, without reimbursement to the inventors of those tests."[46]

Some analysts assert that certain patents, particularly those on research tools[47] in biotechnology, hinder the innovation process. Professors Rebecca Eisenberg and Richard Nelson state that ownership of research tools may "impose significant transaction costs" that result in delayed innovation and possible future litigation.[48] They argue that patents also can stand in the way of research by others:

> Broad claims on early discoveries that are fundamental to emerging fields of knowledge are particularly worrisome in light of the great value, demonstrated time and again in the history of science and technology, of having many independent minds at work trying to advance a field. Public science has flourished by permitting scientists to challenge and build upon the work of rivals.[49]

Professor Arti Rai argues that "the most important research tools are fundamental research platforms that open up new and uncharted areas of investigation" that need further development by researchers in the field.[50] While acknowledging that patent protection on research tools has stimulated private investment in biotechnology and the development of new products and processes, Eisenberg writes that:

> Patents on research tools threaten to restrict access to discoveries that, according to the firm beliefs of scientists trained in the tradition of open science, are likely to have the greatest social value if they are widely disseminated to researchers who are taking different approaches to different problems.[51]

Other commentators dispute these assertions. F. Scott Kieff, then a member of the visiting faculty at Northwestern University School of Law, maintains that there was no such "norm" regarding open scientific access as opposed to intellectual property protection in the basic biological science community.[52] He notes that "experience shows that patents on inputs generally do not prevent the production of outputs" and that the availability of intellectual property protection has expanded the resources available in the biotechnology community and led to its success.[53] Bendekgey and Hamlet-Cox agree that there is no evidence that gene patents have caused a decrease in research as a whole in the biomedical arena or in gene therapies.[54]

A study by Professors John Walsh, Ashish Arora, and Wesley Cohen found little evidence that work has been curtailed due to intellectual property issues associated with research tools.[55] Scientists are able to continue research by "licensing, inventing around patents, going offshore, the development and use of public databases and research tools, court challenges, and simply using the technology without a license (i.e., infringement)." According to the authors, private sector owners of patents permitted such infringement in academia (with the exception of those associated with diagnostic tests in clinical trials) "partly because it can increase the value of the patented technology."

A later analysis by Professors Walsh, Cohen, and Charlene Cho concluded that patents do not have a "substantial" impact upon basic biomedical research and that "none of [their] random sample of academics reported stopping a research project due to another's patent on a research input, and only about 1% of the random sample of academics reported experiencing a delay or modification in their research due to patents."[56] However, obtaining "tangible" research inputs (e.g., actual materials) appear to be more difficult because of competition, cost, and time issues.[57]

CONCLUDING OBSERVATIONS

Congress has exhibited a strong and ongoing interest in facilitating the development of new, innovative pharmaceuticals for the marketplace while reducing the cost of drugs to consumers. To date, the U.S. system of research, development, and commercialization has had a clear impact on the pharmaceutical and biotechnology industries. Policies pertaining to funding for research and development (R&D), intellectual property protection, and cooperative ventures have played an important role in the economic success of these sectors.[58]

A critical component of many of these federal efforts concerns patents.[59] Patent ownership can provide an economic incentive for companies to take the results of research and make the often substantial investment necessary to bring new goods and services to the marketplace. The grant of a patent provides the inventor with a mechanism to capture the returns to his invention through exclusive rights on its practice for a limited time. In the pharmaceutical industry, patents are perceived as particularly important to innovation due, in part, to the ease of duplicating the invention. Now with the decision in *Myriad*, it remains to be seen what the effect may be on research and development in this area and on innovation in the health care arena.

End Notes

[1] 569 U.S. ___, 106 USPQ2d 1972 (2013).
[2] Diamond v. Chakrabarty, 417 U.S. 303 (1980).
[3] See Guyan Lian, "Molecules or Carriers of Biological Information: A Chemist's Perspective on the Patentability of Isolated Genes," 22 Albany Law Journal of Science and Technology (2012), 133.
[4] See, for example, Eileen M. Kane, "Splitting the Gene: DNA Patents and the Genetic Code," 71 Tennessee Law Review (2004), 707.
[5] For example, claim 1 of U.S. Patent No. 5,747,282 recites: "An isolated DNA coding for a BRCA1 polypeptide, said polypeptide having the [following] amino acid sequence...."
[6] 702 F. Supp. 2d 181, 94 USPQ2d 1683 (S.D.N.Y. 2010).
[7] Ibid., at 232, 94 USPQ2d at 1722.
[8] 653 F.3d 1329, 99 USPQ2d 1398.
[9] Ibid., at 1352, 99 USPQ2d at 1415.
[10] 689 F.3d 1323 (Fed. Cir. 2012).
[11] 568 U.S. ___ (2012).
[12] 106 USPQ2d at 1979.
[13] Ibid., at 1980.
[14] Ibid., at 1981.

[15] Ibid.

[16] Ibid.

[17] See Alanna Byrne, "Myriad sues competitors over genetic testing," Inside Counsel (July 11, 2013).

[18] U.S. Patent No. 5,709,999, claim 6.

[19] U.S. Patent No. 5,747,282, claim 6.

[20] U.S. Patent No. 5,753,441, claim 7. Claim 7 is a dependent claim that incorporates claim 1 of the `441 patent, from which the recited language is quoted.

[21] U.S. Patent No. 5,837,492, claim 29.

[22] USPTO, Memorandum from Andrew H. Hirshfeld, Deputy Commissioner for Patent Examination Policy, to the Patent Examining Corps (June 13, 2013) (available at http://www.patentlyo.com/files/myriad_20130613.pdf).

[23] 566 _U.S. _, 132 S. Ct. 1289 (2012). See also CRS Report R42815, Mayo v. Prometheus: Implications for Patents, Biotechnology, and Personalized Medicine, by John R. Thomas.

[24] Michael Crowley, "They Own Your Body," Readers Digest, August 2006, available at http://www.rd.com.

[25] Debra G.B. Leonard, "Medical Practice and Gene Patents: A Personal Perspective," Academic Medicine, December 2002, 1388.

[26] Lori B. Andrews, "Genes and Patent Policy: Rethinking Intellectual Property Rights," Nature Reviews, October 2002, 804.

[27] John F. Merz, "Disease Gene Patents: Overcoming Unethical Constraints on Clinical Laboratory Medicine," Clinical Chemistry, 45:3, 1999, 324.

[28] Medical Practice and Gene Patents: A Personal Perspective, 1388.

[29] Jorge A. Goldstein and Elina Golod, "Human Gene Patents," Academic Medicine, December 2002, Part 2, 1321.

[30] Lee Bendekgey and Diana Hamlet-Cox, "Gene Patents and Innovation," Academic Medicine, December 2002, Part 2, 1378

[31] Iain M. Cockburn, Blurred Boundaries: Tensions Between Open Scientific Resources and Commercial Exploitation of Knowledge in Biomedical Research, April 30, 2005, 15, available at http://people.bu.edu/cockburn/cockburnblurred-boundaries.pdf

[32] Ibid., 11.

[33] "Innovation's Golden Goose," The Economist (US), December 14, 2002, available at http://www.economist.com/ node/1476653?story_id=1476653.

[34] Stuart J.H. Graham, Robert P. Merges, Pam Samuelson, and Ted Sichelman, "High Technology Entrepreneurs and the Patent System: Results of the 2008 Berkeley Patent Survey," Berkeley Technology Law Journal, April 16, 2010, 1255, available at http://www.btlj.org/data/articles/24_feature.pdf.

[35] Richard C. Levin, Alvin K. Klevorick, Richard R. Nelson, and Sidney G. Winter. "Appropriating the Returns for Industrial Research and Development," Brookings Papers on Economic Activity, 1987, in The Economics of Technical Change, eds. Edwin Mansfield and Elizabeth Mansfield (Vermont, Edward Elgar Publishing Co., 1993), 255 and 257.

[36] Wesley M. Cohen, Richard R. Nelson, and John P. Walsh, Protecting Their Intellectual Assets: Appropriability Conditions and Why U.S. Manufacturing Firms Patent (or Not), NBER Working Paper 7552, Cambridge, National Bureau of Economic Research, February 2000, available at http://www.nber.org/papers/w7552.

[37] High Technology Entrepreneurs and the Patent System: Results of the 2008 Berkeley Patent Survey, 1255.

[38] Edwin Mansfield, "Patents and Innovation: An Empirical Study," Management Science, February 1986, 173-181.

[39] Federic M. Scherer, "The Economics of Human Gene Patents," 77 Academic Medicine, December 2002, 1350.

[40] Appropriating the Returns for Industrial Research and Development, 269.

[41] Henry Grabowski, "Patents and New Product Development in the Pharmaceutical and Biotechnology Industries," Duke University Economics Working Paper, July 2002, available at http://www.econ.duke.edu/Papers/Other/ Grabowski/Patents.pdf, 4.

[42] Edwin Mansfield, Mark Schwartz, and Samuel Wagner, "Imitation Costs and Patents: An Empirical Study," The Economic Journal, December 1981, in The Economics of Technical Change, 270.

[43] Patents on Human Genes: An Analysis of Scope and Claims, 1566.

[44] They Own Your Body.

[45] Medical Practice and Gene Patents: A Personal Perspective, 1390.

[46] Gene Patents and Innovation, 1378.

[47] A biotechnology research tool is a cell line, reagent, or antibody used in research.

[48] Rebecca S. Eisenberg and Richard R. Nelson, "Public vs. Proprietary Science: A Fruitful Tension?," Daedalus, Spring 2002.

[49] Ibid.

[50] Arti Rai, "Genome Patents: A Case Study in Patenting Research Tools," Academic Medicine, December 2002, Part 2, 1369.

[51] Rebecca Eisenberg, "Why the Gene Patenting Controversy Persists," Academic Medicine, December 2002, Part 2, 1383.

[52] F. Scott Kieff, "Facilitating Scientific Research: Intellectual Property Rights and the Norms of Science – A Response to Rai and Heisenberg," Northwestern University Law Review, Winter 2001, 694.

[53] Ibid., 704.

[54] Gene Patents and Innovation, 1377, 1378.

[55] John P. Walsh, Ashish Arora, Wesley M. Cohen, "Working Through the Patent Problem," Science, February 14, 2003, 1021.

[56] John P. Walsh, Charlene Cho, and Wesley Cohen, Patents, Material Transfers and Access to Research Inputs in Biomedical Research, September 20, 2005, 37, available at http://tigger.uic.edu/~jwalsh/ WalshChoCohenFinal050922.pdf.

[57] Ibid., 2.

[58] Iain Cockburn, Rebecca Henderson, Luigi Orsenigo, and Gary P. Pisano, "Pharmaceuticals and Biotechnology," U.S. Industry in 2000 (National Academy Press, Washington, 1999), 365.

[59] See CRS Report RL32076, The Bayh-Dole Act: Selected Issues in Patent Policy and the Commercialization of Technology, by Wendy H. Schacht, and CRS Report RL32324, Federal R&D, Drug Discovery, and Pricing: Insights from the NIH-University-Industry Relationship, by Wendy H. Schacht.

In: The Patent System
Editor: Deanna Hoffman
ISBN: 978-1-63482-267-1

Chapter 4

TAILORING THE PATENT SYSTEM FOR SPECIFIC INDUSTRIES*

John R. Thomas

SUMMARY

Congressional interest in the patent system has been demonstrated by the enactment of the Leahy-Smith America Invents Act (AIA) in the 112th Congress. Most of the provisions of the AIA apply to any type of patented invention, whether it consists of a chemical compound, mechanical device, electrical circuit, or other technology. However, other AIA provisions are specific to particular types of inventions, including business methods, tax strategies, and human organisms. The AIA reflects the principle that, for the most part, patentable inventions are generally subject to the same statutory provisions. However, a number of exceptions exist to this concept of technological neutrality.

This blended architecture has for many years prompted inquiry into whether the patent system operates best as a uniform system that applies neutrally to all inventions, or whether it could or should be tailored to meet the specific needs of different industries. Technologies and industrial sectors arguably differ in ways salient to the patent system. Among these distinctions are the costs and risks of research and development, the availability of trade secret protection as an effective

---

* This is an edited, reformatted and augmented version of a Congressional Research Service publication R43264, prepared for Members and Committees of Congress, dated January 14, 2014.

alternative to patenting, the number of patents that cover a particular product, and the patterns of patent acquisition and enforcement of firms within that sector. The patent system involves a number of parameters that could potentially be adjusted to meet the needs of individual sectors, including the speed with which applications are reviewed, the scope of exclusive rights afforded by a patent, and the term of the patent.

While some observers suggest the desirability of sector-specific patent principles, others believe them to be infeasible and unwise. They observe that legislative efforts to define particular industries may prove difficult, that attorneys may sometimes be able to draft patents artfully so as to fall within a favored category, and that U.S. industry is dynamic and resistive to a static statutory definition. In addition, U.S. membership within the World Trade Organization (WTO) may limit the ability to tailor the patent system to account for different industries and inventions, to the extent that compliance with WTO standards is desired. The WTO-administered Agreement on Trade-Related Aspects of Intellectual Property, or TRIPS Agreement, in part requires WTO member states to make patent rights available without discrimination as to the field of technology. The TRIPS Agreement admits some exceptions exist to this principle of technological neutrality, however.

Should Congress believe current circumstances to be appropriate, then no action need be taken. To the degree WTO compliance is desired, Congress could also legislate along the lines permitted by the TRIPS Agreement. Notably, although the TRIPS Agreement generally disallows discrimination with respect to technological fields, it permits distinctions on other grounds. Congress could also make use of regulatory exclusivities and other complementary intellectual property rights that the TRIPS Agreement regulates less heavily.

INTRODUCTION

The recent enactment of the Leahy-Smith America Invents Act (AIA)[1] demonstrates congressional interest in the patent system. Most of the provisions of the AIA apply to any type of patented invention. For example, the first-inventor-to-file priority system,[2] prior user rights,[3] and post-grant and *inter partes* review proceedings[4] apply equally to chemical compounds, electrical appliances, mechanical devices, and any other invention that may be protected by a patent. However, other AIA provisions are specific to particular types of inventions. That statute limited the availability of patents on tax strategies,[5] prohibits the issuance of patents claiming human organisms,[6] and creates "transitional proceedings" that apply exclusively to patents pertaining to business methods.[7] The AIA also allows "prioritization of examination of applications for products, processes, or technologies that are important to the national economy or national competitiveness.... "[8]

The AIA reflects the principle that, for the most part, the U.S. patent system operates in a uniform manner. All patentable inventions are generally subject to the same statutory provisions.[9] A number of exceptions exist to this concept of technological neutrality, however. For example, statutory provisions limit the enforceability of patents claiming methods of medical treatment;[10] call for patent term extension for certain products regulated by the Food and Drug Administration (FDA);[11] and establish specialized patents for designs and plants.[12]

This blended architecture has for many years prompted inquiry into whether the patent system operates best as a uniform system that applies neutrally to all inventions, or whether it could or should be tailored to meet the specific needs of different industries.[13] Commentators have proposed, for example, that software patents should receive shorter terms than patents on other inventions,[14] and that patents on genes should be subject to compulsory licenses that allow individuals to use the patented technology upon paying a license fee.[15] Unenacted legislation in the 112th Congress, H.R. 6245, proposed patent litigation reforms that would apply to patents claiming computer software and hardware, but not to other sorts of inventions.

Notably, U.S. membership in the World Trade Organization (WTO) may influence congressional willingness to promulgate industry-specific patent statutes. One component of the WTO agreements, the Agreement on Trade-Related Aspects of Intellectual Property Rights (TRIPS Agreement),[16] requires patents to be available and enforceable "without discrimination as to ... the field of technology.... "[17] Although the TRIPS Agreement allows for some limited exceptions to this rule of technological neutrality,[18] one consequence of U.S. membership in the WTO may be a restricted ability to tailor the patent statute to particular inventions and industries.[19]

This report considers the possibility of modifying the U.S. patent system to meet the needs of specific industries. After providing a brief review of the patent system, the report identifies different industrial traits, such as the pace of innovation, product cycle, and the cost of research and development, which potentially suggest the desirability of tailored patent rights. It then considers possible points of adjustment within the patent system, including patent term, scope of exclusive rights, and the availability of remedies for infringement. The report then discusses potential difficulties associated with distinguishing among industries within the patent system, including the provisions of the TRIPS Agreement. The report closes with concluding observations.

PATENT FUNDAMENTALS

The patent system covers a broad variety of inventions.[20] U.S. patents cover traditional subject matter such as machines, pharmaceuticals, and manufacturing processes, along with high-tech inventions in the fields of biotechnology, computer software, and nanotechnology. No matter what the sort of technology, however, the patent system in large measure operates under the same general principles.

In particular, all inventors who wish to obtain patent rights must file an application at the U.S. Patent and Trademark Office (USPTO). USPTO examiners then review the application to ensure that certain statutory requirements are met. These statutory requirements—including that the invention be adequately described in the patent application,[21] and that the invention must not have been obvious to a skilled artisan[22]—apply to every invention for which a patent is sought. Similarly, once a patent has issued, the statutory term is set uniformly to 20 years from the date of filing no matter what the type of invention.[23] All patents received the identical exclusive rights—namely, the right to prevent others from making, using, selling, offering to sell, or importing the patented invention in the United States.[24]

Some exceptions exist to this general notion of standardization. The United States has long provided for the protection of industrial designs through so-called "design patents."[25] The Patent Law Treaties Implementation Act of 2012, P.L. 112-211, recently caused U.S. law to conform to the Hague Agreement Concerning the International Registration of Industrial Designs, the leading international agreement on these specialized rights. The United States also established two sorts of intellectual property rights for plants: plant patents, which are administered by the USPTO;[26] and plant variety protection certificates, which are administered by the Department of Agriculture.[27] In addition, the Hatch-Waxman Act extends the terms of patents covering pharmaceuticals, medical devices, and other products which are subject to premarketing approval by the FDA.[28] As well, over the years private legislation has increased the terms of a number of particular patents.[29]

Further, some commentators observe that the statutory provisions for patents are stated fairly generally. In their view, these broad parameters provide courts and the USPTO with some ability to recognize the diverse characteristics of distinct technologies and tailor their rulings accordingly.[30] For example, one core patentability requirement is that the invention must not have been obvious to a person of ordinary skill in the art.[31] The courts have arguably developed nuanced obviousness principles that take into account whether the invention falls within a predictable art, including many mechanical and electrical inventions, as compared to a less predictable art, such as some branches of chemistry and biotechnology. Inventions within these latter, less predictable arts may possibly be more readily able to satisfy the obviousness requirement and therefore are more likely to be patented.[32]

Despite these exceptions, the Patent Act of 1952, as amended by such legislation as the American Inventors Protection Act[33] and AIA, is generally worded in a neutral fashion.[34] The uniform treatment provided by the patent system may be contrasted with the diversity of the technologies and industries to which patents pertain, however, a topic this report takes up next.

THE ROLE OF PATENTS WITHIN DIFFERENT INDUSTRIES

Commentators have for many years recognized that technologies and industries vary in ways that are salient to the patent system. In particular, the costs and risks of conducting R&D differ widely among industries. Arguably the patent incentive should be greater for innovative efforts that are expensive and more likely to fail.[35] Similarly, some sectors are marked by stand-alone, discrete advances, while others feature steady, cumulative innovation. Firms that operate within the latter sorts of industries may have greater need to access technologies invented and patented by others.[36]

As well, product cycles also vary markedly across the U.S. economy. For example, patients may use a particular pharmaceutical for decades, even as consumers quickly discard their old mobile telephones and other electronics in favor of new devices. Industries with compact product cycles may be better served by short application pendency periods at the USPTO and also may be less concerned with lengthy terms of patent protection.[37]

Still another factor may be the practical availability of trade secret protection.[38] Competitors may readily reverse engineer many electrical and mechanical products, for example. Firms within these industries must therefore seek patent rights or enjoy no effective intellectual property rights whatsoever. On the other hand, certain chemical and biotechnology inventions may be more plausibly maintained as trade secrets. Arguably greater encouragement is needed for public disclosure of chemical and biological inventions through the patent system.[39]

The number of patents that cover a particular product also varies widely among industry. Within the pharmaceutical industry, often only a handful, and sometimes only one or two patents cover an individual drug. In contrast, numerous patents may cover a particular electronics product. As RPX Corporation, a self-described "comprehensive patent risk management firm," explains:

> Modern products and services incorporate numerous technology components. The evolution of mobile devices provides an example. Based on our research, we believe there are more than 250,000 active patents relevant to today's smartphones, a significant increase compared to our estimate of approximately 70,000 patents that were active and relevant to mobile phones in 2000. This growth can be attributed to the expanded set of features and functionality incorporated in today's smartphones, including touchscreens, internet access, streaming video, media playback, application store readiness and other web-based services, and WiFi connectivity options.[40]

These "vast disparities in patent-to-product" ratios may influence the perceptions of different business enterprises over the value of individual patents as compared to larger portfolios of intellectual property rights.[41]

Another arguable distinction among industries is the detectability of patents that are pertinent to particular products.[42] Fields such as small-molecule chemistry employ an internationally recognized, standardized nomenclature to identify the composition of a particular compound. As a result, firms within the agricultural, industrial, and pharmaceutical chemical industries may enjoy some confidence that they will be able to identify patents that are relevant to products they wish to sell.[43] In contrast, fields such as software arguably have yet to develop a standardized terminology for identifying programs, procedures, algorithms, and other sorts of machine instructions. The lack of conventions for identifying software inventions potentially impacts the patent system, arguably making the identification of pertinent patents difficult for firms in the computer industry.[44]

IMPLICATIONS FOR THE PATENT SYSTEM

In view of these and possibly other distinctions between technologies and markets, policymakers may not be particularly confident that a one-size-fits-all patent system ideally encourages innovation throughout a diverse array of industries.[45] Observers have for many years suggested that the statute distinguish among the varying inventions and industries for which patents are available. In theory, many aspects of the patent system could be tailored to reflect the needs of distinct technology sectors. Some possible points of adjustment include

- The speed with which the USPTO reviews patent applications could be adjusted to meet the needs of industries with varying product cycles.
- Patents could be more difficult to obtain within some fields than others depending upon the perceived need of the patent incentive to encourage innovation.
- Patents on inventions capable of being protected by trade secrets in whole or in part—for example, biotechnologies or chemical processes—might be required to have more complete technical disclosures in order to allow others to practice the invention expeditiously.
- The term of protection could vary among technologies depending upon the pace of innovation within particular fields.
- The scope of exclusive rights could be adjusted in order to immunize select individuals or enterprises—such as physicians or universities—from liability for patent infringement.
- Compulsory licenses could be made available for categories of patented inventions perceived to fulfill an important public need—for example, healthcare or environmental technologies—thereby allowing third parties to use the invention without the permission of the patent proprietor.

Congress has implemented some of these technology-specific measures. Among other examples, the Hatch-Waxman Act extends the terms of patents covering pharmaceuticals, medical devices, and other products which are subject to premarketing approval.[46] Congress also imposed restrictions upon the enforceability of patents claiming medical procedures.[47] Specialized patent rights exist both for industrial designs and plants.[48]

More recently, the deliberations that led to the enactment of the Leahy-Smith America Invents Act (AIA)[49] again placed focus upon the role of the patent system within different industries. One topic that focused attention upon these distinctions concerned the award of remedies when firms or individuals are found to infringe patents. Broadly speaking, the patent law allows courts to award two sorts of remedies against infringers: (1) injunctions, or court orders requiring an entity to cease future infringements;[50] and (2) damages, consisting of an award of money to compensate patent proprietors for financial losses suffered due to infringements.[51] The legislative history of the AIA reveals that certain representatives of the pharmaceutical and information technology sectors often held different views about the state of the law of patent remedies.[52]

With respect to injunctions, prior to 2006 courts would virtually always enjoin an adjudicated infringer from future practice of the patented invention. Some observers—particularly those from the information technology sector—believed that this "automatic injunction" rule was particularly unfair when the patented invention supported a single function in a multifunctional product, such as an automobile, smart phone, or computer software.[53] They also believed that this rule encouraged the assertion of patents of dubious quality and offered patent proprietors too much leverage during licensing and settlement negotiations.[54] However, other observers—primarily from the pharmaceutical sector—asserted that absent the award of an injunction, competitors would not respect the exclusive rights afforded by a patent.[55]

A predecessor, unenacted version of the AIA, the Patent Reform Act of 2005,[56] proposed changes to the principles governing injunctions in patent law. Section 7 of that bill provided that in deciding whether to issue an injunction or not, "the court shall consider the fairness of the remedy in light of all the facts and the relevant interests of the parties associated with the invention." Perhaps because of the discordant view of different patent stakeholders as to the availability of injunctions in the patent community, this provision was identified as one of the most controversial within the bill.[57]

While debate about congressional action with respect to injunctions in patent law continued, the Supreme Court issued its decision in *eBay Inc. v. MercExchange, L.L.C.* in 2006.[58] There the Court unanimously held that an injunction should not automatically issue based on a finding of patent infringement. Under the *eBay* ruling, courts must weigh equitable factors traditionally used to determine if an injunction should issue, including whether the patent proprietor suffered an irreparable injury; the award of damages would be inadequate to compensate for that injury; that considering the balance of hardships between the patent owner and infringer, an injunction is warranted; and that the public interest would not be disserved by a permanent injunction.[59]

Following the *eBay* decision, Congress did not include legislative provisions concerning injunctive relief in the AIA. Some commentators believe that the Supreme Court struck an appropriate balance by addressing concerns of information technology firms that were concerned that patent holders would assert their rights after the launch of a commercially successful product in an effort to extort an unreasonably large royalty using the threat of an injunction; but also recognized that most often a prevailing patent holder would be awarded an injunction.[60] Further, the early prediction that "the biotech and pharmaceutical industries have little to fear in the post*eBay* world"[61] appears to have been correct, for the great majority of judicial decisions declining the award of a permanent injunction have concerned information technology patents.[62]

A second, arguably divisive issue between the information technology and pharmaceutical industries pertains to damages. Marketplace realities often render the determination of an appropriate damages award a difficult affair in patent litigation. In some cases, the product or process that is found to infringe may incorporate numerous additional elements beyond the patented invention. For example, the asserted patent may relate to a single component of a touch screen display, while the accused product consists of an entire smartphone. In such circumstances, a court may apply "the entire market value rule,"[63] which "permits recovery of damages based upon the entire apparatus containing several features, where the patent-related feature is the basis for consumer demand."[64] On the other hand, if the court determines that the infringing sales were due to many factors beyond the use of the patented invention, the court may apply principles of "apportionment" to reach a just measure of damages for infringement.[65]

Some believe that current damages standards have resulted in the systemic overcompensation of patent owners.[66] Such overcompensation may place unreasonable royalty burdens upon producers of high technology products, ultimately impeding the process of technological innovation and dissemination that the patent system is meant to foster. Others believe that current case law appropriately accounts for apportionment concerns. These observers are concerned that this reform might overly restrict damages in patent cases, thereby discouraging voluntary licensing and promoting infringement of patent rights. Limited damage awards for patent infringement might prevent innovators from realizing the value of their inventive contributions, a principal goal of the patent system.[67]

As discussion of damages reform has proceeded before Congress, the courts have also been active. One of the more notable cases on patent damages principles arose from the efforts of Lucent Technologies, Inc., to enforce its so-called "Day patent," which related to a method of entering information into fields on a computer screen without using a keyboard.[68] In 2002, Lucent brought an infringement suit against computer manufacturer Gateway, Inc., asserting that certain pre-installed Microsoft software infringed the Day patent. At trial, the jury found the Day patent not invalid and infringed. Lucent sought damages of $561.9 million based on 8% of Microsoft's infringing sales, while Microsoft asserted "that a lump-sum payment of $6.5 million would have been the correct amount for licensing the protected technology." The jury then awarded Lucent a single lump-sum amount of $357.7 million.[69]

The litigation in *Lucent v. Gateway* captured the attention of many observers. In a March 3, 2009, letter addressed to Senator Patrick Leahy, Senator Arlen Specter requested a delay in Senate action on the pending patent reform bill until the Federal Circuit heard oral argument in the case.[70] Observing a "symbiotic relationship between the judicial and legislative branches with regard to changes to the patent system," Senator Specter believed that "oral argument has the potential to facilitate a compromise or clarify the applicability of damages theories in various contexts."[71]

In its subsequent decision, the Federal Circuit upheld the lower court's determination that the Day patent was not invalid and infringed. In the most anticipated portion of the opinion, the appellate court also struck down the jury's damages award as not supported by substantial evidence.[72]

Some commentators have viewed the lengthy opinion as doing much to dampen speculative damages awards, particularly with respect to patents from the information technology sector.[73] Following that opinion, Lucent and Microsoft have reportedly settled the litigation.[74] Of broader interest, Congress also chose not to address damages for patent infringement within the AIA.

The timely issuance of *eBay* and *Lucent v. Gateway* may have contributed to congressional belief that courts were appropriately addressing injunctions and damages, respectively. As a result, Congress did not endeavor to reconcile the perceived needs of industries with different innovation and marketplace environments. Another legislative possibility, at least in theory, was to enact distinct remedial rules for different categories of inventions. This report next explores whether industry-specific rules are a practical possibility for patent legislation.

THE FEASIBILITY OF SECTOR-SPECIFIC PATENT RULES

In view of the concerns noted above, commentators have gone so far to say that "it has become increasingly difficult to believe that a one-size-fits-all approach to patent law can survive."[75] To the extent the current patent system creates a blanket set of rules that apply comparably to distinct industries, it likely over-encourages innovation in some contexts and under-incentivizes it in others.[76] Further, some observers have asserted that the need of firms to identify and access the patented inventions of others may differ among industries.[77] As a result, the case can be made that distinct industrial, technological, and market characteristics that exist across the breadth of the U.S. economy compel industry-specific patent statutes.

However, others have questioned the wisdom and practicality of such line-drawing.[78] The following concerns, among others, have been identified:

- Over its long history, the U.S. patent system has flexibly adapted to new technologies such as biotechnology and computer software. Legislative adoption of technology-specific categories may leave unanticipated, cutting-edge technologies outside the patent system.[79]
- Defining a specific industry or category of technologies may prove to be a contested proposition.[80]
- Over time, new industries may emerge and old industries may consolidate. The dynamic nature of the U.S. economy suggests greater need for legislative oversight within a differentiated patent regime.[81]
- Even if an industry or technology remains relatively stable, the innovation environment within it might change. For example, technological or scientific advances might open new possibilities for research and development within hidebound industries—but also increase expense and risk for those firms.[82]
- Distinct patent rights among industries or technologies may lead to strategic behavior on behalf of patent applicants. For example, a computer program that controls a fuel injector within an automobile could possibly be identified as either an automobile-related or a computer-related invention.[83]

- The legislative effort to enact sector-specific patent laws may provide an opportunity for politically savvy firms to exert more lobbying and political power, at the possible expense of less sophisticated firms.[84]

In addition to these practical concerns, U.S. membership in the World Trade Organization (WTO) may restrict congressional ability to tailor the patent system to account for different industries and inventions, to the extent that compliance with WTO standards is desired. The Agreement on Trade-Related Aspects of Intellectual Property Rights (TRIPS Agreement) is a WTO-administered treaty that stipulates minimum standards for many forms of intellectual property protection.[85] Article 27, paragraph one of the TRIPS Agreement expressly provides that, with some exceptions, "patents shall be available and patent rights enjoyable without discrimination as to the place of invention, the field of technology and whether products are imported or locally produced."

At the time it was drafted, the TRIPS Agreement standard of technological neutrality was arguably intended to provide for patent protection for a variety of inventions for which patents were previously unavailable in many countries.[86] For example, certain jurisdictions did not allow patents to issue on pharmaceuticals and agricultural chemicals prior to joining the WTO. The wording of Article 27.1 appears to have broader implications than merely requiring WTO member states to grant patents on pharmaceuticals and other previously unpatentable inventions, however. Its principle of nondiscrimination seems broadly to require that all inventions in all fields of technology be treated identically—a reading that would block, for example, discriminating in favor of particular inventions as well as against them.[87]

Article 27 expressly permits some limited exceptions to this concept of homogeneity. In particular, WTO members may exclude from patentability inventions whose commercial exploitation would violate the public order or morality. However, inventions may not be exempted from patentability merely because their use is illegal.[88] In addition, diagnostic, therapeutic, and surgical methods may also be excluded from patentability.[89] In addition, WTO member states may deny patents on "plants and animals other than micro-organisms, and essentially biological processes for the production of plants or animals other than non-biological and microbiological processes." However, if a WTO member state opts to do so, it must protect plant varieties through an alternative specialized system, typically known as "plant breeder's rights."[90] In addition, the TRIPS Agreement allows for "security exceptions" that permit

WTO members to take any action considered necessary for the protection of "essential security interests."[91]

In addition, Article 30 of the TRIPS Agreement allows for "exceptions to rights conferred." The TRIPS Agreement stipulates that each WTO member state must provide patent proprietors with the right to exclude others from making, using, selling, offering to sell, and importing the patented invention.[92] Article 30 then reads:

> Members may provide limited exceptions to the exclusive rights conferred by a patent, provided that such exceptions do not unreasonably conflict with a normal exploitation of the patent and do not unreasonably prejudice the legitimate interests of the patent owner, taking account of the legitimate interests of third parties.

Article 30 appears to contemplate limited exceptions to the patent rights for such reasons as scientific experiments or use of a patented product for purposes of obtaining regulatory approval.[93]

At first glance, Article 30 of the TRIPS Agreement might seem to provide WTO member states with the ability to provide technology-specific exceptions despite the wording of Article 27.1. However, one dispute settlement panel of the WTO has "concluded ... that the anti-discrimination rule of Article 27.1 does apply to exceptions of the kind authorized by Article 30."[94] Stated differently, the WTO has reasoned that even exceptions to a patent owner's exclusive rights must be technology neutral.

The WTO's conclusion that even exceptions to a patent holder's exclusive rights must operate in a uniform manner has attracted some critical commentary. On one hand, if an exception to a patent holder's exclusive rights must apply to all technologies and industries, it is less likely to be "limited" and therefore compatible with Article 27.1.[95] On the other hand, the WTO reasoned that "the TRIPS Agreement [required] governments to apply exceptions in a nondiscriminatory manner, in order to ensure that governments do not succumb to domestic pressures to limit exceptions to areas where right holders tend to be foreign producers."[96]

The WTO dispute resolution panel in the *Canada Pharmaceutical* case further observed:

> [I]t is not true that Article 27 requires all Article 30 exceptions to be applied to all products. Article 27 prohibits only discrimination as to the place of invention, the field of technology, and whether products are

> imported or produced locally. Article 27 does not prohibit bona fide exceptions to deal with problems that may exist only in certain product areas.[97]

The distinction drawn by the WTO panel between the terms "field of technology" and "certain product areas" arguably does not shimmer with clarity. The panel's opinion obtains no further guidance as to the meaning of "certain product areas." However, some commentators have suggested that patent statutes may permissibly draw distinctions based on narrow categories of goods or services, in contrast to broader fields of technological endeavor. For example, Wesley A. Cann, Jr., an emeritus member of the University of Connecticut business school faculty, has asserted that "[e]ven if Article 30 would not allow a limited exception to be directed at the entire pharmaceutical industry (a position that is still open to substantial doubt), it can be argued that an exception could be made for those particular pharmaceuticals aimed at the prevention and treatment of HIV/AIDS."[98]

As a result, the membership of the United States within the WTO provides a possible constraint against tailoring the patent system to meet the perceived needs of specific industries. To the extent that WTO compliance is desired, the U.S. patent system must ordinarily act in a homogenous manner with respect to particular fields of technology. The TRIPS Agreement does permit some specific exceptions, however, for such subject matter as diagnostic, therapeutic, and surgical methods; matters of national security; and, as explained by the *Canada Pharmaceutical* WTO panel, "certain product areas."

CONCLUDING OBSERVATIONS

The patent system involves numerous parameters, including the requirements to obtain a patent, the scope of proprietary rights, and the term of protection. In theory these attributes could be tailored to meet the needs of different sectors. Defining industry-specific or technology-specific patent doctrines presents some practical difficulties, however, and may also give rise to incompatibilities with the WTO TRIPS Agreement.

Should Congress consider current circumstances with respect to the patent system to be appropriate, then no action need be taken. However, should Congress believe that different sectors possess distinctive needs with respect to the patent system, a number of options exist. As noted, the TRIPS Agreement provides for a number of limited exceptions to the general rule of technological neutrality. U.S. legislation could simply track the exceptions identified by the provisions of the TRIPS Agreement, with particular reference to their interpretation by WTO dispute resolution panels.

Congress could also potentially draw distinctions among grounds not identified by Article 27.1 of the TRIPS Agreement—namely, the place of invention, the field of technology, and whether products are imported or produced locally. For example, the Leahy-Smith America Invents Act (AIA) established an infringement defense based upon the prior commercial use of the patented invention by the accused infringer.[99] The AIA stipulated that this defense was unavailable if the patented invention was made by an institution of higher education, however.[100] This "university exception" appears to comply with the TRIPS Agreement because it draws a distinction based upon the identity of the inventor, rather than on a ground identified in Article 27.1.

Another option is the establishment of additional intellectual property rights that complement patents. For example, Congress has established so-called "regulatory exclusivities," a term that refers to a period of time during which a regulated product is afforded protection from competing applications for marketing approval.[101] Most notably, the food and drug laws establish a number of regulatory exclusivities that apply to pharmaceuticals and are administered by the Food and Drug Administration. In contrast to patents, regulatory exclusivities are not subject to extensive regulation by the TRIPS Agreement.[102] As a result, at least with respect to regulated industries, regulatory exclusivities may provide a more flexible instrument for legislative tailoring of intellectual property rights.[103]

Whether legal doctrines should be expressed as discrete rules or more generally phrased standards is a long-standing debate within the field of jurisprudence.[104] Placed within the context of congressional consideration of our intellectual property laws, the debate suggests that distinct rules for different sectors form one possibility for patent reform. Yet Congress may also craft broader principles that may be appropriately applied across the diverse industries and technologies to which the patent system pertains. Determining whether a rule or a standard provides the most appropriate vehicle for a particular reform to our patent laws remains a matter of legislative judgment.

End Notes

[1] P.L. 112-29, 125 Stat. 284 (2011). See CRS Report R42014, The Leahy-Smith America Invents Act: Innovation Issues, by John R. Thomas.
[2] Ibid. at §3.
[3] Ibid. at §5.
[4] Ibid. at §6.
[5] Ibid. at §14.
[6] Ibid. at §33.
[7] Ibid. at §18.
[8] Ibid. at §25.
[9] Clarisa Long, "Our Uniform Patent System," 55 The Federal Lawyer (2008), 44.
[10] 35 U.S.C. §287(c).
[11] 35 U.S.C. §156.
[12] 35 U.S.C. §§161, 171.
[13] Michael W. Carroll, "One Size Does Not Fit All: A Framework for Tailoring Intellectual Property Rights," 70 Ohio State Law Journal (2009), 1361.
[14] Mark H. Webbink, "A New Paradigm for Intellectual Property Rights in Software," Duke Law & Technology Review (2005), 12.
[15] Daniel M. Lorentzen, "Do These Genes Fit? Genes as Patentable Subject Matter," 60 Drake Law Review (2012), 933.
[16] Agreement on Trade-Related Aspects of Intellectual Property Rights, April 15, 1994, Marrakesh Agreement Establishing the World Trade Organization, Annex 1C, 1869 U.N.T.S. 299 (1994).
[17] Ibid. at Art. 27.
[18] Ibid.
[19] Dan L. Burk & Mark A. Lemley, "Is Patent Law Technology-Specific?," 17 Berkeley Technology Law Journal (2002) 1155.
[20] 35 U.S.C. §101 (patents available on machines, manufactures, compositions of matter, and processes).
[21] 35 U.S.C. §112(a).
[22] 35 U.S.C. §103.
[23] 35 U.S.C. §154(a)(2).
[24] 35 U.S.C. §271(a).
[25] 35 U.S.C. §171-173.
[26] 35 U.S.C. §§161-164.
[27] 7 U.S.C. §§2321-2582.
[28] 35 U.S.C. §156. See CRS Report R41114, The Hatch-Waxman Act: Over a Quarter Century Later, by Wendy H. Schacht and John R. Thomas.
[29] See CRS Report RS21129, Pharmaceutical Patent Term Extensions: A Brief Explanation, by Wendy H. Schacht and John R. Thomas.
[30] Dan L. Burk and Mark A. Lemley, "Policy Levers in Patent Law," 89 Virginia Law Review (2003), 1575.
[31] 35 U.S.C. §103(a).
[32] See Briana Barron, "Structural Uncertainty: Understanding the Federal Circuit's Lead Compound Analysis," 16 Marquette Intellectual Property Law Review (Summer 2012), 401.
[33] P.L. 106-113.

[34] Michael W. Carroll, "One for All: The Problem of Uniformity Cost in Intellectual Property Law," 55 American University Law Review (2006), 845.

[35] For discussion of how the features of a patent system might pertain to R&D costs, see Robert M. Hunt, "Economics and the Design of Patent Systems," 13 Michigan Telecommunications & Technology Law Review (Spring 2007), 457.

[36] See Mark A. Lemley, "The Myth of the Sole Inventor," 110 Michigan Law Review (2012), 709 (discussing how cumulative innovation witnessed in many industries may impact patent law principles).

[37] See Sarah A. Geers, "Common Sense and the Fact Finder Without Skill in the Art: The Role of Objective Evidence in Achieving Proper Technology Specificity," 40 Seton Hall Law Review (2010), 425 (discussing patent system design in relation to distinct industry product cycles).

[38] See CRS Report R41391, The Role of Trade Secrets in Innovation Policy, by John R. Thomas.

[39] For a general discussion of the relationship between patents and trade secrets, see J. Jonas Anderson, "Secret Inventions," 26 Berkeley Technology Law Journal (2011), 917.

[40] See Daniel O'Connor, "One in Six Active U.S. Patents Pertain to the Smartphone," Disruptive Competition Project (October 17, 2012) (available at http://www.project-disco.org/intellectual-property/one-in-six-active-u-s-patentspertain-to-the-smartphone/).

[41] Graeme B. Dinwoodie and Rochelle C. Dreyfuss, "Diversifying Without Discriminating: Complying with the Mandates of the TRIPS Agreement," 13 Michigan Telecommunications & Technology Law Review (2007), 445.

[42] See James Bessen and Michael J. Meurer, Patent Failure: How Judges, Bureaucrats, and Lawyers Put Innovation at Risk (Princeton University Press 2008), 46-72.

[43] See Christa J. Laser, "A Definite Claim on Claim Indefiniteness: An Empirical Study of Definiteness Cases of the Past Decade with a Focus on the Federal Circuit and the Insolubly Ambiguous Standard," 10 Chicago-Kent Journal of Intellectual Property (2010), 25.

[44] Ibid.

[45] Dan L. Burk and Mark A. Lemley, "Is Patent Law Technology-Specific?," 17 Berkeley Technology Law Journal (2002) 1155.

[46] 35 U.S.C. §156.

[47] 35 U.S.C. §287(c).

[48] 35 U.S.C. §§171-173 (designs); 35 U.S.C. §§161-164 (plants).

[49] P.L. 112-29, 125 Stat. 284 (2011).

[50] 35 U.S.C. §283.

[51] 35 U.S.C. §284.

[52] See CRS Report RL33367, Patent Reform: Issues in the Biomedical and Software Industries, by Wendy H. Schacht.

[53] See Lea Shaver, "Illuminating Innovation: From Patent Racing to Patent War," 69 Washington & Lee Law Review (2012), 1891.

[54] Nicholas P. Chan, "Balancing Judicial Misvaluation and Patent Hold-Up: Some Principles for Considering Injunctive Relief After Ebay," 59 UCLA Law Review (2012), 746.

[55] Paul M. Schoenhard, "Who Took My IP? Defending the Availability of Injunctive Relief for Patent Owners," 16 Texas Intellectual Property Law Journal (2008), 187.

[56] H.R. 2795, 109th Congress.

[57] George H. Pike, "The Next Step in Patent Reform," 28 Information Today no. 10 (November 1, 2011), 1.

[58] 547 U.S. 388 (2006).

[59] See Mark P. Gergen et al., "The Supreme Court's Accidental Revolution: The Test for Permanent Injunctions," 112 Columbia Law Review (2012), 203.

[60] William C. Rooklidge and Alyson G. Barker, "Reform of a Fast-Moving Target: The Development of Patent Law Since the 2004 National Academies Report," 91 Journal of the Patent and Trademark Office Society (2009), 153.

[61] Michael Beylkin, "Much Ado About Nothing: The Biotech and Pharmaceutical Industries Have Little to Fear in the Post-eBay World," 6 Journal of Telecommunications & High Technology Law (2007), 179.

[62] See University of Houston Law Center, PatStats: U.S Patent Litigation Statistics (available at http://www.patstats.org).

[63] LaserDynamics, Inc. v. Quanta Computer, Inc., 694 F.3d 51 (Fed. Cir. 2012).

[64] State Industries, Inc. v. Mor-Flo Industries, Inc., 883 F.2d 1573 (Fed. Cir. 1989).

[65] See LaserDynamics v. Quanta, supra.

[66] See Amy L. Landers, "Let the Games Begin: Incentives to Innovation in the New Economy of Intellectual Property Law," 46 Santa Clara Law Review (2006), 307.

[67] See William C. Rooklidge, "Reform of the Patent Laws: Forging Legislation Addressing Disparate Interests," 88 Journal of the Patent and Trademark Office Society (2006), 9.

[68] Lucent Technologies, Inc. v. Gateway, Inc., 580 F.3d 1301 (Fed. Cir. 2009).

[69] Ibid. at 1308.

[70] The letter is available at http://www.fr.com/files/uploads/attachments//patentdamages//03-03-09-Specter-to-PJLPatents.pdf.

[71] Ibid.

[72] 580 F.3d at 1335.

[73] See Bo Zeng, "Lucent v. Gateway: Putting the "Reasonable" Back into Reasonable Royalties," 26 Berkeley Technology Law Journal (2011), 329.

[74] "Microsoft and Alcatel-Lucent Settle Patent Dispute," Computer News Middle East (January 19, 2012).

[75] Dreyfuss and Dinwoodie, supra.

[76] See Alan Devlin, "Patent Law's Parsimony Principle," 25 Berkeley Technology Law Journal (2010), 1693.

[77] See Alan Devlin, "Systematic Bias in Patent Law," 61 DePaul Law Review (2011), 57.

[78] See Luigi Orsenigo and Valerio Sterzi, Comparative Study of the Use of Patents in Different Industries, Knowledge, Internationalization and Technologies Studies Working Paper 33/2010 (2010).

[79] Ibid.

[80] See Lewis Kaplow, "Why (Ever) Define Markets?," 124 Harvard Law Review (2010), 437.

[81] Burk and Lemley, supra.

[82] Orsenigo and Sterzi, supra.

[83] See Kristen Osenga, "The Shape of Things to Come: What We Can Learn About Patent Claim Length," 28 Santa Clara Computer & High Technology Law Journal (2012), 617.

[84] Burk and Lemley, supra.

[85] Agreement on Trade-Related Aspects of Intellectual Property Rights, April 15, 1994, Marrakesh Agreement Establishing the World Trade Organization, Annex 1C, 1869 U.N.T.S. 299, 33 I.L.M. 1197 (1994).

[86] See Robert Weissman, "A Long, Strange Trips: The Pharmaceutical Industry Drive to Harmonize Global Intellectual Property Rules, and the Remaining WTO Legal Alternatives Available to Third World Countries," 17 University of Pennsylvania Journal of International Economic Law (1996), 1069.

[87] See Rebecca S. Eisenberg, "The Role of the FDA in Innovation Policy," 13 Michigan Telecommunications & Technology Law Review (2007), 345.

[88] TRIPS Art. 27.2.

[89] Ibid. at Art. 27.3(a).

[90] Ibid. at Art. 27.3(b).

[91] Ibid. at Art. 73.

[92] Ibid. at Art. 28.

[93] See Scott Taylor, "Where Are the Green Machines? Using the Patent System to Encourage Green Invention and Technology Transfer," 23 Georgetown International Environmental Law Review (2011), 577.

[94] Panel Report, Canada-Patent Protection of Pharmaceutical Products, WT/DS114/R (March 17, 2000) (hereinafter "Canada Pharmaceutical").

[95] See Dinwoodie and Dreyfuss, supra.

[96] Canada Pharmaceutical, paragraph 7.92.

[97] Ibid.

[98] Wesley A. Cann, Jr., "On the Relationship Between Intellectual Property Rights and the Need of Less-Developed Countries for Access to Pharmaceuticals: Creating a Legal Duty to Supply Under a Theory of Progressive Global Constitutionalism," 25 University of Pennsylvania Journal of International Economic Law (2004), 755.

[99] P.L. 112-29, 125 Stat. 284 (2011), at §5.

[100] Ibid. (establishing 35 U.S.C. §273(e)(5)).

[101] See Yaniv Heled, "Patents vs. Statutory Exclusivities in Biological Pharmaceuticals—Do We Really Need Both?," 18 Michigan Telecommunications & Technology Law Review (2012), 419.

[102] See Christina Bucci, "Responsible Patent Protections: Preserving Public Health Objectives in the Trans-Pacific Partnership Agreement," 26 Pacific McGeorge Global Business & Development Law Journal (2013), 213.

[103] See Eisenberg, supra.

[104] See David Olson & Stefania Fusco, "Rules Versus Standards: Competing Notions of Inconsistency Robustness in Patent Law," 64 Alabama Law Review (2013), 647.

In: The Patent System
Editor: Deanna Hoffman
ISBN: 978-1-63482-267-1

Chapter 5

AN OVERVIEW OF THE "PATENT TROLLS" DEBATE*

Brian T. Yeh

SUMMARY

Congress has recently demonstrated significant ongoing interest in litigation by "patent assertion entities" (PAEs), which are colloquially known as "patent trolls" and sometimes referred to as "non-practicing entities" (NPEs). The PAE business model focuses not on developing or commercializing patented inventions but on buying and asserting patents, often against firms that have already begun using the claimed technology after developing it independently, unaware of the PAE patent. PAEs include not only freestanding businesses but patent holding subsidiaries, affiliates, and shells of operating companies that want to participate in the PAE industry and/or a new means of countering competitors. The proliferation of PAEs was among the central factors raised in support of the most recent patent reform legislation, the Leahy-Smith America Invents Act of 2011 (AIA). However, the AIA contains relatively few provisions that arguably might impact PAEs, apparently because of lively debate over what, if anything, should be done about them. In the 113th Congress, the Saving High-Tech Innovators from Egregious Legal Disputes (SHIELD) Act of 2013 (H.R. 845) has been introduced in an effort to affect the number of lawsuits filed by PAEs.

---

* This is an edited, reformatted and augmented version of Congressional Research Service, Publication No. R42668, dated April 16, 2013.

PAEs emerged alongside the burgeoning tech industry around the turn of the 21st century and gained notoriety with lawsuits claiming exclusive ownership of such ubiquitous technologies as wireless email, digital video streaming, and the interactive Web. They have had the attention of Congress, the press, and the public since at least 2006, when a successful PAE suit almost caused the shutdown of BlackBerry wireless service. Such victories in court are rare for PAEs; they lose 92 percent of merits judgments. But few cases make it that far. The vast majority of defendants settle because patent litigation is risky, disruptive, and expensive, regardless of the merits; and many PAEs set royalty demands strategically well below litigation costs to make the business decision to settle an obvious one. For most PAEs, the costs of litigating and losing are more than offset by the licensing fees they can gain by demonstrating their tenacity to future defendants.

According to one estimate, PAEs generated $29 billion in direct costs from defendants and licensees in 2011, a 400 percent increase over $7 billion in 2005, and some researchers suggest these costs are primarily deadweight, with less than 25 percent flowing to support innovation and at least that much going towards legal fees. Another study reported that 62% of all patent suits filed in 2012 were brought by PAEs. Critics assert that PAEs undermine the purposes of patent law—promoting innovation by providing incentives to invest in development and commercialization of inventions—and injure companies that play a vital role in the American economy. However, defenders of PAEs argue that they actually promote invention by adding liquidity options, managing risk, and compensating small inventors. The Federal Trade Commission and several leading scholars suggest that these benefits exist but are significantly less than the costs they impose. What remains unclear is the extent of imbalance between costs and benefits and whether Congress could recalibrate it to advance the goals of patent law while avoiding unintended consequences.

This report reviews the current debate and controversy surrounding PAEs and their effect on innovation, examines the reasons for the rise in PAE litigation, and explores the legislative options available to Congress if it decides that these are issues that should be addressed.

INTRODUCTION

Congress has recently demonstrated significant ongoing interest in the issue of “patent assertion entities” (PAEs), which are popularly referred to as “patent trolls.” The Leahy-Smith America Invents Act of 2011 (AIA) included an order for further study of PAE litigation,[1] and in March 2013, the House

Judiciary Subcommittee on Courts, Intellectual Property and the Internet held a hearing on "abusive patent litigation" and PAEs.[2] Furthermore, in July 2012, both the House and the Senate held hearings regarding patent disputes at the International Trade Commission (ITC), which has seen a surge in patent complaints as federal courts have become less patent holder-friendly after passage of the AIA in 2011 and a landmark Supreme Court ruling in 2006.[3] The much-publicized proliferation of PAEs was among the central factors that prompted the AIA,[4] but at the end of the day, Congress passed a few provisions arguably addressing PAEs while leaving several other PAE-related issues unresolved, apparently in light of lively debate over what, if anything, should be done about them.

The PAE business model focuses not on developing or commercializing technologies but on buying and asserting patents against companies that have already begun using them, often after independently developing them without knowledge of the PAE's patent, according to a report by the Federal Trade Commission (FTC).[5] PAEs emerged alongside the burgeoning tech industry around the turn of the 21st century and gained notoriety with lawsuits claiming exclusive ownership of such ubiquitous technologies as wireless email, digital video streaming, and the interactive Web.[6] They have had the attention of Congress, the press, and the public since at least 2006, when a successful PAE suit almost caused the shutdown of BlackBerry wireless service.[7]

Such victories in court are rare for PAEs. According to one empirical study, they lose 92 percent of merits judgments,[8] but few cases make it that far. The vast majority end in settlements because litigation is risky, costly, and disruptive for defendants, and PAEs often offer to settle for amounts well below litigation costs to make the business decision to settle an obvious one.[9]

Observers expect that the AIA will reduce the volume of meritless lawsuits, but not dramatically. While the provisions for post-grant examination and transitional scrubbing of business method patents will help with assertions of invalid patents, they do not address the supposed use of *valid* patents to extract undue royalties from defendants that are either locked in to the patented technology or not infringing the patent at all. Additionally, post-grant examination is not available for patents granted prior to the AIA, and the AIA's restrictions on joinder do not apply in a case brought before the ITC (thus, PAEs could still name multiple parties as respondents in a single ITC complaint even if they have no relation to each other).

Reform advocates fear that PAEs impede innovation, undermine the patent system, and wreak havoc on businesses that play a vital role in the American economy. According to one study, PAE activity cost defendants and licensees $29 billion in 2011, a 400 percent increase over $7 billion in 2005, and the losses are mostly deadweight, with less than 25 percent flowing to innovation and at least that much going towards legal fees.[10] Another recent study suggests that PAE activity could harm competition to the extent that operating companies use or "sponsor" PAEs as a means of imposing costs on rivals and achieving other anticompetitive ends.[11]

Defenders of PAEs argue that they actually promote invention by increasing the liquidity and managing the risk of investments in applied research and invention, as well as by compensating small inventors.[12] PAEs' strongest allies include universities and other non-practicing entities that benefit from having PAEs as buyers for their patents and are not as vulnerable to lawsuits because they ordinarily do not make or sell anything that could be infringing.[13] Other defenders of the status quo raise concerns about unintended consequences and collateral effects of changes to the law.

The Federal Trade Commission and numerous scholars suggest that PAE activity does indeed have beneficial effects but that, under current law, these benefits are significantly outweighed by the costs.[14] What remains unclear is the extent of the imbalance between costs and benefits and whether Congress should attempt to rebalance any disparity. In Section 34 of the AIA, Congress instructed the Government Accountability Office to study the costs, benefits, and consequences of litigation by "non-practicing entities" and "patent assertion entities" and report back with findings and recommendations on how to "minimize any negative impact" of such litigation.[15]

This report reviews the current debate and controversy surrounding PAEs, examines the reasons for the rise in PAE litigation, and explores the legislative options available to Congress if it decides that PAEs are an issue that should be addressed.

PATENT LAW FUNDAMENTALS

Patent law finds its constitutional basis in Article I, Section 8, Clause 8, of the U.S. Constitution[16] and its statutory basis in the Patent Act of 1952.[17] Patents provide the right to exclude others from making, using, selling, or importing claimed inventions for a limited period of time, generally 20 years. Inventors may acquire patents by submitting an application to the U.S. Patent and Trademark Office (PTO), where officials will examine it to determine whether the statutory requirements are met. This process is commonly known as "prosecution."

Applications consist of "claims" establishing the metes and bounds of the patent property right, which is typically broader than the specific invention, and a "specification" that describes the claimed invention. The specification must be detailed and concrete enough to enable others to make and use the invention without undue experimentation.[18] Claims must consist of a patentable subject matter—"any new and useful process, machine, manufacture, or any composition of matter, or any new and useful improvement thereof"—rather than abstract ideas or law of nature, and satisfy substantive requirements of novelty, nonobviousness, and utility.[19]

The patent holder may enforce its rights by filing infringement suits in federal court against anyone who makes, uses, sells, or imports the patented technology, regardless of whether it was copied or developed independently.[20] Courts presume that patents granted by the PTO are valid, but accused infringers may introduce evidence of invalidity or unenforceability. The patent holder bears the burden of establishing infringement by each alleged infringer.[21] Patent litigation is very expensive;[22] the average suit in which $1 million to $25 million is at stake costs $1.6 million through discovery and $2.8 million through trial.[23]

Upon a finding of infringement, a federal court may issue an injunction if doing so seems more equitable than simply awarding monetary damages. The statute also provides for the award of damages "adequate to compensate for the infringement, but in no event less than a reasonable royalty for the use made of the invention by the infringer."[24] The U.S. Court of Appeals for the Federal Circuit has national jurisdiction over most patent appeals from the district courts.[25]

A patent holder can also enforce its rights by filing a complaint with the International Trade Commission (ITC), which may issue an exclusion order blocking importation of the infringing product into the United States.[26] The ITC is not authorized to issue damages, however.[27]

THE "PATENT TROLLS" CONTROVERSY

Skyrocketing rates of patent litigation since the turn of the 21st century have often been tied to the rise of "patent assertion entities" (PAEs),[28] businesses modeled on "purchasing and asserting patents against manufacturers who may be using the technology" rather than developing or commercializing the technologies themselves.[29] They are frequently accused of being classic arbitrageurs, taking advantage of the "large gap between the cost of getting a patent and the value that can be captured with an infringement action" in the information technology (IT) sector.[30]

PAEs are frequently referred to as "patent trolls," after the villains of folklore known to lie in wait under bridges they did not build, then emerge from the smog to demand tolls from unsuspecting travelers.[31] The term "troll" is controversial because it is both pejorative and ambiguous, often used imprecisely for any opportunistic or unpopular patent holder.[32] But it is best understood as an epithet for PAEs, which object to the label and argue essentially that the fees they collect are legitimate and needed to fund investment in infrastructure—that if they did not take tolls, bridges would be fewer in number and lower in quality.

Enforcement by PAEs

PAEs seek to license their patents primarily *ex post facto*—often after defendants have independently invented and begun using a technology allegedly covered by their patents, and frequently only after it has become ubiquitous or standard-essential in an industry.[33]

Indeed, the average patent asserted by the most litigious PAEs is not litigated for the first time, or assigned to its final owner, until seven years into its term, according to a study by Professor Michael Risch.[34] By contrast, product firms tend to assert their patents early in the patent term, and Professor Brian J. Love finds that the gap in litigation timing is such that "the average product-company patent has been shelved by its owner before the average NPE patent has even been asserted."[35]

PAEs suggest that they simply enforce patent property rights against infringers, but much of the controversy surrounding their activities comes from the impression that they lack valid claims to the royalties they demand and receive.[36] Studies suggest that PAEs rarely prevail on the merits. Their win rate in cases decided on the merits is just 8 percent, versus 40 percent for other entities, according to a study by Professors John R. Allison, Mark A. Lemley, and Joshua Walker.[37] But they persist with litigation nonetheless, apparently supported by the licensing fees obtained by posing a credible threat of extended litigation.[38]

Contrary to popular belief, however, PAEs do not lose more because their patents are weaker or more likely to be invalid, according to Villanova University Law Professor Michael Risch.[39] In fact, he finds the patents asserted by the most litigious PAEs to be on par with other patents by objective measures of quality and value, and no studies supports the idea that they are especially prone to invalidation, relative to other patents.[40] Rather, PAEs often fail to show infringement, perhaps because they seek and depend upon overly broad constructions of what their patent claims cover.[41]

PAEs vs. Other Non-Practicing Entities

PAEs describe themselves as critical intermediaries. Some claim to offer "department stores" for patents, providing one-stop shopping for licensing and purchase.[42] Others suggest they serve key functions by enabling individual inventors, who generate about 12% of patents,[43] to earn returns despite lacking the resources to enforce or commercialize their patents themselves.[44]

No one doubts that an efficient patent system needs intermediaries who reduce transaction costs between those who invent things and those who develop and commercialize them. Many observers note, however, that PAEs "do not seem to operate that way,"[45] and that other non-practicing entities (NPEs) serve these functions more efficiently and without "trolling" tactics.[46] PAEs are alleged to be one-of-a-kind in that they are said to speculate on patents—they bet on how much more a patent will be worth in the future, when it is asserted, and focus on high-risk high-yield acquisitions.[47]

Other NPEs with licensing-based business models include technology development firms and licensing agents, but PAEs differ from these in that they generally offer licenses only after infringement and lock-in have begun.[48] The FTC explained that while other NPEs transfer technologies that they or their clients invented and developed so that licensees can benefit from not having to develop them in-house, PAEs transfer nothing but a legal right not to be sued for using a technology that the licensee may have already invested in developing on its own, without help from the PAE or its patents.[49] PAEs also diverge from other NPEs that *enforce* patents because they focus on acquiring patents outright and asserting them on their own behalf, as opposed to providing services and collecting fees or a slice of the litigation award.[50]

The Impact on Innovation

PAEs have frequently been accused of imposing a "tax on innovation" and undermining or impairing the incentives that patent law aims to create. Yet PAEs have also been defended on the grounds that they actually promote invention by adding liquidity, absorbing some of the risk otherwise borne by investors, and getting more royalties for small inventors.[51] Without a doubt, PAEs both add to and subtract from the incentives of patent law,[52] but the FTC and many experts in the field indicate that they currently do more harm than good to innovation and the patent system.[53] The extent of this imbalance—and whether Congress could or should recalibrate it to "support the beneficial effects, and lessen the detrimental ones"—remains unclear, however.[54]

To the extent that PAEs wait to seek licenses until defendants have sunk costs into a product or invested in developing a disputed technology on their own, the FTC suggests that they can deter innovation by raising costs and risks for the companies and investors that actually bring products to market.[55] Investment decisions must factor in the likelihood that PAEs will later emerge and demand royalties or bring costly litigation,[56] directly reducing returns on investment.[57] Faced with lower profit margins and uncertain but potentially significant risk, manufacturers may find that some R&D projects, features, and product improvements are simply not worth doing, even if beneficial to consumers. Similarly, startups and small businesses may have a harder time getting funding from venture capitalists and other investors who anticipate future PAE demands.

There are also opportunity costs as productive entities divert funds from R&D to deal with PAEs. In addition to the obvious diversion to pay licensing fees and legal costs, there has also been a shift towards investing in PAEs instead of startups or other ventures. Some investors buy stakes in PAEs to hedge against the limitless risk of being sued by PAEs—strengthening them to deal with the damage they may experience elsewhere.[58] One high-tech entrepreneur explained that "[i]f patent laws continue to be as they are, this is the only way I can see that allows any level of protection."[59] Other investors have simply realized that PAEs offer great returns on investment— better than many startups—and shifted funding in their direction.[60]

On the other hand, PAEs argue they actually promote investment in invention. Nathan Myhrvold, CEO of PAE giant Intellectual Ventures, styles his company as pioneering a "capital market for inventions akin to the venture capital market that supports start-ups and the private equity market that revitalizes inefficient companies."[61] The most recognized benefit of PAE activity is increased liquidity and better risk management for investments in applied research and invention. By enlivening a secondary[62] market for patents, PAEs provide an exit option and/or extra revenue stream for a variety of patentees. They absorb and manage the high risk[63] by spreading it across large portfolios of patents and extracting value out of otherwise low-value or dormant patents.

Patentees who do not or cannot commercialize in the "primary" market for technology[64] might recoup their costs and perhaps see some returns by selling their patents to PAEs and retaining a cut of future royalties. PAEs suggest this function is especially essential for small inventors and NPEs that would otherwise have a hard time getting any value from their inventions.

NPEs that routinely obtain and sell patents in the secondary market—universities in particular— benefit directly from, and in proportion to, PAE activity.[65] The more licensing fees PAEs obtain, the more these inventors earn from their patents, and the greater their incentives to invent.[66]

The FTC, however, warns that an increase in the volume of inventions attributable to PAEs should not be taken as a trump card: "Paying inventors only to invent and patent may generate more *invention and patents*, but it may not generate more *innovation*. Invention is only the first step in a lengthy and expensive development process to bring an innovation to market."[67]

PAEs may create disincentives for firms to invest in the rest of the process to turn inventions into products and bring them to market. The more a firm invests in R&D, the more likely it is to be sued by a PAE.[68] And each extra dollar PAEs pay out for patents in the secondary market may deduct from the profits of firms that actually commercialize and make use of patented technologies.

James Bessen and Michael J. Meurer have reported that of the $29 billion PAEs cost defendants in 2011, no more than 25 percent of it flowed back to innovation—the rest they categorize as deadweight loss.[69] In other words, this report calculated that only a fraction of defendant losses go towards the benefits PAEs assert.

Empirical research has also raised doubts about how much PAEs actually help small inventors and startups. Another Bessen-Meurer study indicated that *less than two percent* of losses in wealth caused by PAEs passed through to independent inventors,[70] which according to other studies supply only 29 percent of PAE patents; 43 percent come from large firms.[71] PAEs also impose costs upon small- and mid-sized businesses, which comprised 90 percent of defendants sued by PAEs in 2011 and bore 37 percent of the direct costs, according to Bessen and Meurer.[72]

BEHIND THE RISE OF PAES

Experts attribute the proliferation of PAEs over the past 10 to 15 years to the explosion of the information technology (IT) industry and patent law's struggle to adapt to the unique issues presented by this new frontier of innovation. They indicate that the PAE business model is not about licensing patents generally but *high-tech* patents in particular,[73] including those on software and business methods or processes related to software, as well as computers and electronics.[74]

Why do high-tech patents attract and enable PAEs? First, inadvertent infringement is said to be inevitable due to notice failure and the so-called "patent thicket," among other things. Second, uneven bargaining power enables PAEs to negotiate excessive royalties from infringers and undue royalties from non-infringers. The high value that can be extracted from patents that have been plausibly or actually infringed, together with the relatively low cost of acquiring and warehousing them, invites arbitrage.[75]

Notice Failure

There is virtually universal agreement that "notice failure" in the IT sector has contributed to the rise of PAEs, as well as the rise in patent litigation generally. In an optimal patent regime, patent property rights are clearly defined and easily determined so the world is on notice as to their existence, scope, and ownership.[76] This "notice function" enables people to avoid infringement, negotiate permission to use others' IP, and maximize efficiency, such as by not keeping all inventions as trade secrets or doing R&D on inventions already claimed by someone else.[77]

The relative success of the patent system for pharmaceuticals has been linked in part to a manageable volume of clearly defined claims.[78] By contrast, the notice function has broken down in the IT sector. There are two aspects to notice failure: (1) claims have "fuzzy boundaries" that cannot be reliably determined, much less known in advance, without litigation;[79] (2) it is economically infeasible or irrational for defendants to search through existing patents to avoid infringement.

Section 112 of the Patent Act

Several provisions of §112 are supposed to filter out abstract or ambiguous patents and ensure the world is on notice as to what each patent covers. The FTC and many observers indicate that these requirements have been less stringently applied and enforced in the IT industry than other sectors where notice failure is less of a problem.

First, the "definiteness" requirement limits the ambiguity of the patent "claim" language, which establishes the metes and bounds of the patent property right.[80] Claims must "particularly point[] out and distinctly claim[] the subject matter which the applicant regards as his invention."[81] Yet critics say the provision has had no teeth since 2001,[82] when the Federal Circuit replaced a test requiring claims to be "plain on their face" with one under which claims are only invalid for indefiniteness if "insolubly ambiguous" and subject to "no narrowing construction."83 The test, deemed a "disaster" by some,[84] dramatically widened the "zone of uncertainty which enterprise and experimentation may enter only at the risk of infringement claims."[85]

Second, the boundaries set by the patent claims are sharpened by looking at the accompanying disclosures, which according to the FTC should explain what the claims cover in a more detailed and concrete way so as to clarify ambiguities around the outer edges that may exist or arise later.[86] It must include a specific "written description" of the claimed invention and enough explanatory details to "enable" others in the field to make and use it.[87] Here, too, observers assert that IT patents undergo less stringent review than other types of patents, and some suggest that this permits more abstract patents and inventions that exist only on paper.[88] If §112 rules are loosely enforced and ambiguity does not put patents at risk of later invalidation, patentees may have less incentive to write definite claims and concrete, detailed disclosures (because every detail added may cabin their patent property right later).[89]

The Patent Thicket

According to commentators, several conditions in the IT sector make it economically and/or practically infeasible or irrational for manufacturers to find and clear all patents incorporated in a given product. They report that, as a result, in most cases, "the first notice of the patent [is] the filing of the lawsuit," at which point it is too late to design around the technology or negotiate a reasonable royalty rate because the producer has become locked in.[90] The leverage this gives to PAEs will be discussed further below. This section explains why it is often said that virtually all IT products inadvertently infringe some patent(s) and why the industry has apparently taken to ignoring patents altogether.[91]

Commentators indicate the IT sector is mired in what they call a "patent thicket," meaning a "dense web of overlapping [IP] rights that a company must hack its way through . . . to actually commercialize new technology."[92] According to many observers, the set of potentially relevant patents for any IT product is overwhelming due to both the number of (overlapping and possibly invalid) patents *granted* in this area and the number of components *incorporated* in each product.[93]

Even for products with relatively few patents to review, commentators indicate that their "fuzzy boundaries" would still make it a futile endeavor, and under the doctrine of willful infringement, a risky one.[94] That doctrine has been criticized for creating perverse disincentives by exposing defendants who looked at patents they are later found to infringe to enhanced damages, adding to the cost, risk, and duration of litigation.[95] If those issues were addressed, a full search would still entail huge costs for marginal returns, insuring against neither infringement nor litigation.

Even the most thorough search will leave some stones unturned—those pending at the PTO.[96] Between the application and issuance dates, patent claims cannot be accessed or checked by other firms, which meanwhile might develop and market infringing products. Strategic use of continuation practice to keep patents pending and hidden longer at the PTO has become an increasingly common and criticized practice.[97]

Finally, clearing the patent thicket does nothing to prevent weak or baseless suits brought only to extract a settlement from the defendant. Recall that PAEs lose 92 percent of merits judgments and settle the vast majority of their assertions.[98] These figures may be attributable to uneven bargaining power, which is the subject of the next section.

Uneven Bargaining Power

PAEs occupy highly advantageous bargaining positions, and their leverage over defendants has been attributed to an asymmetry of costs and risk that breaks down into three factors: high litigation costs and no way to dispose of weak suits early; the risk of potentially debilitating liability for defendants; and the lack of any major risk or disincentive for PAE plaintiffs to litigate.

First, patent litigation is expensive, and there is no quick or affordable way to get rid of a patent suit except to settle.[99] Defendants frequently find settlement the most cost-effective option, even if they are certain that they are not infringing.[100] The AIA provisions increasing the speed and availability of post-grant examination is expected to ameliorate this issue somewhat for invalid patents granted after 2011. Defendants will be able to challenge a patent's validity, but not its scope or the claim of infringement, at a much lower cost than they can in court, where they must overcome a presumption of validity by clear and convincing evidence to get a patent invalidated.[101]

Second, where injunctive relief is available to PAEs, what commentators call the "patent holdup" problem arises as PAEs leverage the threat of an injunction in royalty negotiations to "capture far more than the intrinsic value of their invention."[102] Those wielding this power have described it as a "Damocles sword."[103] Patent holdup is said to be particularly acute in the IT sector because products incorporate dozens or even thousands of patented features or components, and the owner of any one of them can keep the entire product off the market.[104]

In 2006, the Supreme Court took a step towards fixing the so-called holdup problem with its decision in *eBay v. MercExchange*, which enabled lower courts to deny injunctive relief to PAEs and issue only monetary damages for infringement.[105] The case overturned a longstanding "general rule" of the Federal Circuit that injunctions issue automatically upon a finding of infringement.[106] Courts now apply a four-factor balancing test that tends to weigh against PAEs. Indeed, few injunctions have been granted in patent infringement cases since *eBay*.[107]

Scholars have raised concerns that PAEs have now shifted their holdup efforts to the International Trade Commission (ITC), a quasi-judicial federal agency that grants "exclusion orders" that stop the import of infringing products into the United States.[108] The ITC has responded to the concerns with data showing that just 8 percent of post-*eBay* ITC investigations arose from complaints by PAEs, only one of which obtained an exclusion order.[109] But both sides may be correct if, as the scholars suggest, each of the PAE complaints ensnares entire industries by asserting that industry standards, adopted and incorporated by all manufacturers, infringe their patents.[110]

Third, by contrast to their targets, PAEs have nothing to lose and much to gain by litigating aggressively. Unlike most other patentee-plaintiffs, PAEs pursuing infringement suits "do not risk disruption to their core business" because "patent enforcement *is* their core business."[111]

Because PAEs are NPEs that do not make or sell anything, they are not subject to counterclaims that they infringe on defendants' patents. By contrast, when a product firm sues another firm for infringement, the defendant can dig up or acquire a patent that the plaintiff's products might infringe and counterclaim. The resulting dynamic of mutual assured destruction makes bargain power more even, settlement more likely, and litigation far less appealing. Compounding that leverage, the PAE business model creates unusual incentives for PAEs to forge ahead with weak suits (rather than calling it a loss or accepting a lowball settlement) to reinforce their bargaining position with future targets. The ability to extract licensing fees depends upon posing a credible threat of costly litigation.

PAEs also have less to lose than other plaintiffs if a patent is invalidated or narrowly construed. Although PAEs lose future revenue when a lucrative patent is invalidated, this cannot deter them from litigating because the whole value of a PAE's patents depends upon its demands being backed by a credible threat of litigation. Additionally, by the time a validity judgment comes down, the PAE will often have already extracted royalties from other defendants, and these licensing and settlement agreements are often one-time, non-refundable deals.[112]

The joinder limitations included in the America Invents Act might reduce the leverage PAEs can exert. Section 19 of the AIA restricts the ability to sue multiple unrelated defendants for infringement in the same case or same trial "based solely on allegations that they each have infringed the patent or patents in suit,"[113] which had become a common practice among PAEs.[114] PAEs must now incur more costs per defendant they sue and face multiple assessments of validity, each with potential collateral estoppel effect. Commentators have predicted that Section 19 will have an impact but not a tremendously significant one, potentially reducing the number of defendants getting sued while increasing the number of suits filed.[115] But if the threat of litigation that gives force to a PAE's licensing demands becomes less credible because it cannot follow through with suing all firms that refuse to buy a license, then its leverage is reduced.

LEGISLATION IN THE 113TH CONGRESS

On February 27, 2013, Representatives Peter DeFazio and Jason Chaffetz introduced the Saving High-Tech Innovators from Egregious Legal Disputes (SHIELD) Act of 2013 (H.R. 845), which is intended to make PAEs responsible for paying alleged infringers' court costs and attorney's fees if they lose their infringement case in court. A previous version of the SHIELD Act had been introduced in the 112th Congress but did not see action.[116] The Patent Act currently provides a court with the power to award reasonable attorney's fees to the prevailing party "in exceptional cases."[117] The SHIELD Act of 2013 would amend the Patent Act by inserting a new section 285A, which would require a court, in an action involving the validity or infringement of a patent, to award full litigation costs (including reasonable attorney's fees) to the prevailing party asserting that the patent is invalid or not infringed, if the court determines that the party alleging infringement does ***not*** meet one or more of the following three conditions:

1. The party is the inventor, joint inventor, or the original assignee of the patent;
2. The party can provide evidence of substantial investment made by the party in the exploitation of the patent through production or sale of an item covered by the patent; or
3. The party is an institution of higher education or is a technology transfer organization whose primary purpose is to facilitate commercialization of technology developed by such institution.[118]

Thus, the legislation attempts to specifically target PAE litigants by providing a "negative definition" of a PAE (though it never explicitly uses such term); a party that does not satisfy any one of the conditions listed above would be liable to the alleged infringer for full litigation costs, if the party loses the lawsuit. The SHIELD Act would require the party asserting invalidity or noninfringement to file a motion with the court requesting a judgment that the adverse party does not meet any one of the above conditions. Within 120 days of such motion, the court would need to make a determination as to whether the adverse party meets at least one of these conditions.[119] If the adverse party fails to meet a condition, the party would be required to post a bond in an amount set by the court to cover the alleged infringer's litigation costs, should the court ultimately find that the adverse party's patent is invalid or not infringed.[120]

As Representative Chaffetz explained in introducing the bill, "Patent trolls contribute nothing to the economy. No industry is immune to these attacks. Instead of creating jobs and growing the economy, businesses are wasting resources to fight off frivolous lawsuits. This bipartisan legislation will curb future abuse by requiring trolls to bear the financial responsibility for failed claims."[121]

Some have criticized the SHIELD Act for not providing additional explanation about the phrase "substantial investment ... in the exploitation of the patent"; they have also pointed out that a PAE could try to meet that particular condition in order to avoid paying the litigation costs:

> [W]hat does "substantial" mean? Presumably it is intended to ensnare NPEs that decide to make things, but not make enough (or good enough) things. But why should a court get to decide what is enough? And what do we do about start-ups who have patents but have not yet commercialized their invention? Are they trolls, too?
>
> And what is to stop NPEs from becoming distributors? They could buy competing products wholesale (perhaps products where they have secured licenses) and sell them. This only makes sense; by being resellers, they can claim that the competition of the infringing product is harming their sales business.[122]

Other commentators have questioned how the SHIELD ACT's bond requirement would work in practice:

> How would the "full costs" amount of the required bonds be determined at the beginning of each, separate suit, when different defendants will employ different defense strategies, and incur different "full costs"? Will the bond amount be the subject of legal opinions of counsel, or of expert opinions? What banks, sureties, or insurance companies would offer to provide SHIELD Act bonds to NPEs? Assuming that some financial institutions would, in fact, offer to provide SHIELD Act bonds, what amount and type of collateral would be required and, more importantly, how would typically asset-free, judgment-proof NPEs provide that collateral?[123]

OTHER LEGISLATIVE OPTIONS

Commentators have suggested a number of legislative avenues to address PAE activity.

IT-Specific Reform

It bears emphasis that PAE activity has been concentrated in the realm of IT, primarily on patents related to software, the Internet, and electronics.[124] Due to the component-driven and intangible nature of IT, as well as indications that patents are less essential to promoting innovation in IT than in other industries, such as pharmaceuticals, some observers urge Congress to undertake targeted reforms and leave the other realms of the patent system as they are.[125] This could entail distinctions based on type of patent or the industry area, an approach already taken by the SHIELD Act.

However, such precision may be precluded, or at least constrained, by an international agreement. Article 27.1 of the Agreement on Trade-Related Aspects of Intellectual Property Rights ("TRIPS"), administered by the World Trade Organization (WTO), requires that patents "be available and patent rights enjoyable without discrimination as to ... the field of technology."[126] But some observers have argued that this provision "does not strictly require a 'single level of IP protection for all technologies or industries.'"[127] In fact, a WTO panel "rejected a strict interpretation of Article 27.1 prohibiting any differentiation between fields of technology," and the "accepted view is that 'the pejorative concept of discrimination must be distinguished from differentiation for *legitimate reasons*.'"[128] Nevertheless, Congress may need to carefully examine whether any changes it desires to make to the patent system would be inconsistent with its international obligations.

Improving Notice

Improving notice where it currently fails is a relatively uncontroversial and high-priority goal of some patent reform advocates. The "fuzzy boundaries" of IT patents and the sheer number of them that are granted and incorporated in any given product make it difficult for firms to avoid infringement and, once faced with a PAE assertion, to know whether it is valid without going to court. There are also a number of disincentives and obstacles for product firms to find and clear patents ahead of time. Many scholars believe solving this notice failure would go far towards reducing the negative effects of PAEs while keeping the benefits and making the entire patent system work better.[129]

Among the most popular ideas is more robust use of §112's definiteness and disclosure rules to deny (at the PTO) or invalidate (in court) abstract or ambiguous IT patents,[130] which may entail legislatively overruling Federal Circuit standards that permit "substantial ambiguity" in IT patent claims.[131] Of course it is also an option to let the Federal Circuit sort these matters out itself.

For definiteness, Congress might consider amendments that point the Federal Circuit to a test that "weeds out claims reasonably susceptible to multiple interpretations," which the FTC says "could reduce ambiguity and improve notice in a broad range of settings."[132] Many observers want a test that weeds out more claims than the "insolubly ambiguous" standard adopted by the Federal Circuit in 2001.[133] Others believe current doctrine is adequate but underenforced.[134]

Several reform proposals address the issue of patent applicants keeping claims hidden at the PTO by filing continuations. The most common among them involve reforms of continuation practice, which currently "allows patent owners to hide the true nature of their invention until late in the process" and extend the time during which other companies might unknowingly begin using the patented technology.[135] There have also been many calls for the PTO to make pending applications more open to the outside world so that there are no surprises and more assurance for diligent companies that do search for existing patents.

Finally, some scholars propose eliminating what they view as a disincentive for firms to search existing patents in advance. The "willfulness doctrine"[136] is said to boost PAE bargaining power and has the "perverse effect of causing people to try avoid learning of patents."[137] Congress might consider legislation that would delay the ability to even plead willfulness until there has been a finding of infringement.[138] Proponents argue this would preserve the doctrine's deterrent and punitive functions while improving notice and removing a tool PAEs use to raise defendants' costs and risk, as well as their own bargaining power.[139]

Reducing Leverage, Hold-Up, and Settlement Pressure

The leverage PAEs can exert by threatening an injunction from a federal court has diminished since the Supreme Court decided *eBay* in 2006, but commentators now indicate that PAEs have replaced it with the "Damocles sword" derived from credibly threatening to get an ITC exclusion order on the import of defendants' products.[140] Congress recently heard testimony urging it to prevent the ITC from issuing exclusion orders for PAEs and is currently considering action to that effect.[141] As noted above, PAEs play a smaller role in the growth of ITC complaints than reformers seem to believe,[142] *but* it is possible that PAEs have extracted royalties by threatening ITC import bans and rarely needed to actually file.

Other procedural changes that shift more of the burdens and costs of litigation onto PAEs could also reduce their bargaining leverage over defendant product companies. Some scholars have called upon Congress to eliminate the presumption of validity, now given to patents out of deference to the PTO.[143] Currently rebuttable only by "clear and convincing evidence," the presumption increases costs for defendants and leverage for PAEs.[144] It might also extend the use of an invalid patent and the number of defendants a PAE can assert it against.

Another common suggestion is to change royalty calculation rules, which often provide damages "disproportionate" to the contribution of the infringed patent as a portion or component of the overall product.[145] Critics posit that in the IT sector, "if every patented portion of an invention was licensed at the same rate as the infringed patent, the inventor would face a net loss."[146] The 110th and 111th Congresses considered legislation to address this issue, but nothing was passed.[147] Observers indicate that IT interests support such changes due to the many components in each of their products while pharmaceutical, biotechnology, and NPE or PAE interests have opposed it.[148] Congress could consider IT-specific royalty reforms.

Escalating Costs or Diminishing Rights Over Time

Many changes proposed by scholars target the practice of sitting on a patent until infringement and/or lock-in to a plausibly infringing technology have occurred and only then notifying targets of the patent and offering them licenses. One idea that has been floated is to decrease the patent period for IT patents, which are quickly outdated yet litigated aggressively through the end of their 20-year terms.[149] A forthcoming study by Brian J. Love shows that it may be that a shorter term would primarily harm PAEs:[150]

> Product companies predominately enforce their patents soon after they issue and complete their enforcement activities well before their patents expire. NPEs,[151] on the other hand, begin asserting their patents relatively late in the patent term and frequently continue to litigate their patents to the verge of expiration. Indeed, I find that the average product-company patent has

been shelved by its owner before the average NPE patent has even been asserted.[152]

NPEs account for the majority of suits brought in the final three years of the patent term,[153] and the product firms that litigate late in the term are "a unique group of companies that . . . blur the line between practicing entities and trolls."[154] Love's study also finds that high-tech patents represent an outsized portion of patents litigated in the last three years of their terms, comprising 86 percent for NPEs and 72 percent for product firms, even though most 18- or 20-year-old software patents are likely outdated.[155]

An alternative to shortening the patent term would involve changes to the maintenance fees that patent holders pay at certain points in the patent term to keep their rights in force.[156] Fees could escalate over the life of the patent or increase with each renewal and apply across the board or just for inactive patents, entities with big portfolios, or IT-related patents. Another possibility is cost- and burden-shifting in the latter half of the patent term.

Consequences for Dormancy

Under other variations, patent owners could face repercussions if they neglect to engage in bona fide use, development, or licensing of their patents for a set number of years.[157] The conditions triggering such effects might be modeled after that for trademark "abandonment" under the Lanham Act: non-use with the intent not to use in the reasonably foreseeable future.[158]

Not practicing a patent for a number of years could be prima facie evidence of abandonment that patent owners would have to rebut before any infringement suit could proceed. Evidence of efforts to develop, commercialize, or license the patent would rebut the prima facie assumption as long as they are both bona fide—not taken "merely to reserve a right"—and done in good faith. Ex post licensing would not qualify as a use, and availability through a designated clearinghouse of some kind might be required.[159]

As for the effect triggered by the period of non-use, options range from cancellation to the shifting of costs and burdens onto PAEs, diminishing their leverage and increasing their costs. Other ideas include removing the presumption of validity, subjecting plaintiffs to heightened pleading and production requirements, or freezing the patent until the patent owner begins to use it.

Patent Market

A leading scholar and a leading PAE have partnered to advocate consideration of another reform: requiring publication of patent assignment and license terms.[160] Mark Lemley of Stanford Law School and Nathan Myhrvold of Intellectual Ventures point out that patents currently exist in an inefficient blind market.[161] The publication requirement would not solve the uncertainty and notice issues, but:

> [I]t will permit the aggregate record of what companies pay for rights to signal what particular patents are worth and how strong they are, just as derivative financial instruments allow market to evaluate and price other forms of risk. It will help rationalize patent transactions, turning them from secret, one-off negotiations into a real, working market for patents. And by making it clear to courts and the world at large what the normal price is for patent rights, it will make it that much harder for a few unscrupulous patent owners to hold up legitimate innovators, and for established companies to systematically infringe the rights of others.[162]

Lemley and Myhrvold anticipate concerns that patent holders would not license their patents if they had to disclose the licenses but suggest that this is a less a problem than people might think, concluding that "[t]he only people who stand to lose from mandatory disclosure of licenses are those who are taking advantage of the current state of ignorance."[163]

End Notes

[1] *See* Leahy-Smith America Invents Act, P.L. 112-29, §34 (2011) (instructing the GAO to study PAE litigation and report back on costs, benefits, and consequences, and how to minimize any negative impact).

[2] *Abusive Patent Litigation: The Impact on American Innovation & Jobs, and Potential Solutions: Hearing Before the H. Subcomm. on Courts, Intellectual Prop. and the Internet*, 113th Cong. (2013).

[3] eBay, v. MercExchange, L.L.C., 547 U.S. 388 (2006); *The Int'l Trade Comm'n and Patent Disputes: Hearing Before the H. Subcomm. on Intellectual Prop., Competition, and the Internet*, 112th Cong. (2012) [hereinafter "ITC House hearing"]; *Oversight of the Impact on Competition of Exclusion Orders to Enforce Standard-Essential Patents, Hearing Before the S. Judiciary Comm.*, 112th Cong. (2012) [hereinafter "ITC Senate hearing"].

[4] *See, e.g., Patent Trolls: Fact or Fiction?: Hearing Before the Subcomm. on Courts, the Internet, and Intellectual Prop. of the H. Comm. on the Judiciary*, 109th Cong. (2006).

[5] FEDERAL TRADE COMMISSION, THE EVOLVING IP MARKETPLACE: ALIGNING PATENT NOTICE AND REMEDIES WITH COMPETITION 50–51 (2011) [hereinafter FTC Report].

[6] *See* Gerard N. Magliocca, *Blackberries and Barnyards: Patent Trolls and the Perils of Innovation*, 82 NOTRE DAME L. REV. 1809 (2007).

[7] *Id.*

[8] John R. Allison, Mark A. Lemley & Joshua Walker, *Patent Quality and Settlement Among Repeat Patent Litigants*, 99 GEO. L.J. 677, 694 (2011).

[9] *Id.*

[10] *See* James Bessen & Michael J. Meurer, *The Direct Costs from NPE Disputes* 18–19 (Boston Univ. School of Law, Law and Economics Research Paper No. 12-34, 2012). *But see* David L. Schwartz and Jay P. Kesan, *Analyzing the Role of Non-Practicing Entities in the Patent System* (Chicago-Kent College of Law Research Paper No. 2012-03, 2012) (criticizing the methodology used by Bessen & Meurer).

[11] *See generally* Tom Ewing, *Indirect Exploitation of Intellectual Property Rights By Corporations and Investors*, 4 HASTINGS SCI. & TECH. L.J. 1 (2011); *see also* FTC Report, *supra* note 4.

[12] *See, e.g.,* Ron Epstein, *Debunking the 'Patent Troll' Myth*, BLOOMBERG BUSINESSWEEK, August 15, 2011, *available at* http://www.businessweek.com/stories/2010-02-01/debunking-the-patent-troll-mythbusinessweek-business-newsstock-market-and-financial-advice.

[13] *See* Mark A. Lemley, *Are Universities Patent Trolls?*, 18 FORDHAM INTELL. PROP. MEDIA & ENT. L.J. 611, 618 (2008).

14 *See generally* FTC Report, *supra* note 4; James Bessen et. al., *The Private and Social Costs of Patent Trolls*, REGULATION 26 (2006).

[15] P.L. 112-29, §34 (2011).

[16] U.S. CONST. art. I, §8, cl. 8 ("To promote the Progress of ... useful Arts, by securing for limited Times to ... Inventors the exclusive Right to their ... Discoveries. . .").

[17] P.L. 82-593, 66 Stat. 792 (codified at 35 U.S.C.).

[18] 35 U.S.C. §112 (2012).

[19] 35 U.S.C. §101 (2012).

[20] 35 U.S.C. §271 (2012).

[21] 35 U.S.C. §271 (2012).

[22] ALAN R. THIELE ET. AL., THE PATENT INFRINGEMENT LITIGATION HANDBOOK 125 (2010).

[23] AMERICAN INTELLECTUAL PROPERTY LAW ASSOCIATION, 2011 REPORT OF THE ECONOMIC SURVEY (2012).

[24] 35 U.S.C. §284 (2012).

[25] 28 U.S.C. §1295 (2012).

[26] 19 U.S.C. §1337 (2012).

[27] *Id.*

[28] There is no consensus on a less-loaded synonym for "patent troll" as it is most commonly understood, but "PAE" has recently become the choice of both Congress and the FTC. *See* FTC Report, *supra* note 4, at 60–61; ITC House and Senate Hearings, *supra* note 2. The most popular alternative choice is "non-practicing entity" (NPE), but that term is too broad, ensnaring universities and fledgling inventors. Research organization Patent Freedom defines NPEs as companies receiving most of their revenue from patent licensing or enforcement—which is how this report defines PAEs—but that usage is confusing because

it does not align with the intuitive or common meaning of "NPE." *See* PATENT FREEDOM, WHAT IS AN NPE?, https://www.patentfreedom.com/about-npes/background (last visited July 20, 2012). PAEs bring most NPE suits. Allison et. al., *supra* note 7, at 684. According to one estimate, PAEs filed 62% of all patent lawsuits in 2012. RPX Corporation, *Tracking PAE Activity: A Post-script to the DOJ Review*, at http://www.rpxcorp.com/index.cfm?pageid=14&itemid=29.

[29] *See* FTC Report, *supra* note 4, at 67–68.

[30] Magliocca, *supra* note 5, at 1812.

[31] The term was coined at Intel in 2001 as a pithy label for litigants asserting patents that they owned but did not practice and which they typically acquired. An Intel Corporation vice president had been sued after referring to such litigants as "patent extortionists." *See* Joff Wild, *The Real Inventors of the Term "Patent Troll" Revealed*, IAM MAGAZINE, August 22, 2008, http://iam-magazine.com/blog/detail.aspx?g=cff2afd3-c24e-42e5-aa68-a4b4e7524177.

[32] *See, e.g.*, Ronald S. Katz et. al., *Patent Trolls: A Selective Etymology*, IP LAW 360, March 20, 2008, http://manatt.com/uploadedFiles/News_and_Events/Articles_By_Us/patentroll.pdf.

[33] FTC Report, *supra* note 4, at 50–51. Standard-essential patents claim technologies that have been adopted as industry-wide standards by standard-setting organizations. *Id.* at 191–92.

[34] Michael Risch, *Patent Troll Myths*, 42 SETON HALL L. REV. 457, 490 (2012).

[35] Brian J. Love, *An Empirical Study of Patent Litigation Timing: Could a Patent Term Reduction Decimate Trolls Without Harming Innovators?* 3 (SSRN Working Paper Series 2011), http://ssrn.com/abstract=1917709.

[36] *See* Risch, *supra* note 34, at 459.

[37] Allison et. al., *supra* note 7, at 694.

[38] *See* AMERICAN INTELLECTUAL PROPERTY LAW ASSOCIATION, *supra* note 23.

[39] *See* Allison et. al., *supra* note 7, at 706.

[40] *See* Risch, *supra* note 33, at 481.

[41] *Id.*

[42] Nathan Myhrvold, *The Big Idea: Funding Eureka!*, HARV. BUS. REV. 44 (2010).

[43] JAMES BESSEN AND MICHAEL J. MEURER, PATENT FAILURE 169 (2008).

[44] *See* Myhrvold, *supra* note 41, at 48–49; Sannu K. Shrestha, *Trolls or Market-Maker? An Empirical Analysis of Nonpracticing Entities*, 110 COLUM. L. REV. 114, 126–30 (2010); FTC Report, *supra* note 4, at 64, 68.

[45] *See* Robin Feldman & Tom Ewing, *The Giants Among Us*, 2012 STAN. TECH. L. REV. 1, 20–21 (2012).

[46] *See, e.g.*, Bessen et. al, *supra* note 13, at 34; Elizabeth D. Ferrill, *Patent Investment Trusts: Let's Build a PIT to Catch the Patent Trolls*, 6 N.C. J.L. & TECH. 367, 371–374 (2005).

[47] *Id.*; Steven M. Cherry, *Patent Profiteers*, IEEE SPECTRUM, June 2004, at 38–41; FTC Report, *supra* note 4, at 62–67; Raymond Millen & Ron Laurie, *Meet the Middlemen*, INTELL. ASSET MGMT. 54 (2008).

[48] Development firms, such as Qualcomm, focus on research and development of technologies, rather than acquisition of patents, and then pitch their patented technologies to licensees in advance. Licensing agents, meanwhile, offer enforcement and negotiation services without acquiring or asserting patents on their own behalf. *See* Cherry, *supra* note 46, at 38–41; FTC Report, *supra* note 4, at 62–67.

[49] FTC Report, *supra* note 4, at 40 n. 43.

[50] Ferrill, *supra* note 45, at 371–374.

[51] *See* Myhrvold, *supra* note 41, at 44–45.

[52] *See* FTC Report, *supra* note 4, at 67–68.

[53] *See* FTC Report, *supra* note 4, at 67–68.; Love, *supra* note 34.

[54] It is worth noting that the asserted benefits of PAE activity tend to be more long-term, abstract, and indirect, and thus more difficult to estimate.

[55] *See* FTC Report, *supra* note 4, at 52–54; Bessen et. al., *supra* note 13, at 31–35 (finding the risk of future lawsuit-related losses to be a large disincentive to invest in innovation that far exceeds counterbalancing incentives).

[56] *See* FTC Report, *supra* note 4, at 52–54; Bessen et. al., *supra* note 13, at 31–35; *see also* Eric Savitz, *Cuban Says Vringo Stake Hedges Patent Risk In Other Investments*, FORBES, April 17, 2012.

[57] *See* FTC Report, *supra* note 4, at 52–54; Bessen et. al., *supra* note 13, at 31–35.

[58] When an outspoken advocate for patent reform bought a stake in a company known to "aggressively sue over IP," he explained, "This is a hedge against the unlimited patent exposure all the companies I have investments in face. Patent risk is impossible to quantify. It's unrealistic for most small to medium businesses to have any clue which patents they are at risk over." Mark Cuban, *The Greatest Business Risk You Don't Know About*, BLOG MAVERICK, April 18, 2012, http://blogmaverick.com/2012/04/18/the-greatest-business-risk-you-dont-know-about-yourbusiness-will-be-sued-over-patents.

[59] Jay Yarow, *Mark Cuban: Here's Why I'm Taking A Big Stake in A Patent Troll*, BUS. INSIDER, April18, 2012, http://articles.businessinsider.com/2012-04-18/tech/31359139_1_patent-suit-patent-troll-patent-laws#ixzz1zmuCpoFR.

[60] *See* House ITC Hearing, *supra* note 2 (statement of Colleen V. Chien).

[61] *See* Nathan Myhrvold, *supra* note 41, at 41–42.

[62] In the *primary* market for *technology*, revenue and returns on investment come from commercializing the patented technology and exploiting exclusive rights to use it in the marketplace. In the *secondary* market for *patents*, revenue comes from licensing fees. PAEs sell or license their patents "as assets whose values are based on the amount of licensing fees that can be extracted from operating companies already using and marketing the technology." *See* FTC Report, *supra* note 4, at 60.

[63] Some suggest that only 1 to 3 percent of patents turn profits for their inventors, Myhrvold, *supra* note 41, at 46, and that only 7 percent even recoup the costs of their prosecution. Michael Agger, *Google Patent Overload*, SLATE, January 2, 2007, http://www.slate.com/id/2156386/fr/flyout.

[64] Smaller inventors may lack the resources or know-how to commercialize, and it will often be inefficient for them to try. Other patents may not become valuable for years or require further capital and sunk costs.

[65] Repeat-seller NPEs such as universities are unique because they which benefit greatly from selling to PAEs but never bear the costs on the other side (in the form of licensing fees and litigation costs). *See* Lemley, *supra* note 12, at 618. The Bayh-Dole Act empowered universities to reap revenue benefits from their applied research and patenting activities, but it is a point of contention whether it adds to incentives, or if it does, whether they are the right kind. *Id.*

[66] *Id.*

[67] *See* FTC Report, *supra* note 4, at 69 (emphasis added).

[68] *See* Bessen et. al., *supra* note 13, at 34; Colleen V. Chien, *Of Trolls, Davids, Goliaths, and Kings: Narratives and Evidence in the Litigation of High-Tech Patents*, 87 N.C. L. REV. 1571, 1581 (2009).

[69] Bessen et. al., *supra* note 13; Bessen & Meurer, *supra* note 9.

[70] Bessen et. al., *supra* note 13, at 32–33.

[71] Risch, *supra* note 33, at 459–61.

[72] Bessen & Meurer, *supra* note 9, at 19.

[73] PAE suits are concentrated in the IT sphere, with about 64% of NPE-asserted patents coveting computer- or electronics-related inventions, and almost 40% covering software-related inventions. They also account for 40 to 60 percent of suits over high-tech patents. *See* Bessen, *supra* note 9; Magliocca, *supra* note 5, at 1812; Chien, *supra* note 67; Love, *supra* note 34.

[74] *See, e.g.*, Bessen et. al., *supra* note 13, at 34; ARTICLE ONE PARTNERS, *Strategies for a Shifting IP Landscape: A Summary of Summit Takeaways*, 2011 (reporting that NPEs brought 75 percent of all active litigation matters reported by a non-random sample of leading firms).

[75] Drawing on historical parallels and the concentration of opportunistic litigation around certain types of patents, Magliocca has concluded that "opportunistic licensors flourish when there is a large gap between the cost of getting a patent and the value that can be captured with an infringement action." Magliocca, *supra* note 5, at 1812.

[76] BESSEN & MEURER, *supra* note 42, at 10; FTC Report, *supra* note 4, at 3–8.

[77] BESSEN & MEURER, *supra* note 42, at 10.

[78] *Id.*

[79] *See* FTC Report, *supra* note 4, at 9–12. Among the reasons not discussed here: the inherent limitations and imprecision of language, especially for emerging inventions; the lack, in fields such as software, of "clear nomenclatures and common vocabularies"; the possibility that claims viewed narrowly at the PTO will be construed broadly by courts; and the PTO's focus on novelty and nonobviousness rather than clear claim boundaries. *Id.*

[80] Dan L. Burk & Mark A. Lemley, *Is Patent Law Technology-Specific?*, 17 BERKELEY TECH. L.J. 1155, 1188 (2002) (explaining that definiteness requires claims to be "written so as to warn members of the public just what is and is not covered by the patent"); FTC Report, *supra* note 4, at 10–11.

[81] 35 U.S.C. §112.

[82] FTC Report, *supra* note 4, at 95.

[83] *See* Exxon Research & Eng'g Co. v. United States, 265 F.3d 1371, 1375 (Fed. Cir. 2001).

[84] *See* FTC Report, *supra* note 4, at 95.

[85] FTC Report, *supra* note 4, at 94 (quoting United Carbon Co. v. Binney & Smith Co., 317 U.S. 228, 236 (1942)).

[86] *See* FTC Report, *supra* note 4, at 94–95.

[87] 35 U.S.C. §112.

[88] *See* Chien, *supra* note 67, at 1581; Bessen et. al., *supra* note 13, at 34.

[89] *See* Bessen et. al., *supra* note 13, at 34.

[90] FTC Report, *supra* note 4, at 59 n. 36.

[91] *See generally* Mark A. Lemley, *Ignoring Patents*, 2008 MICH. ST. L. REV. 19 (2008).

[92] Carl Shapiro, *Navigating the Patent Thicket: Cross Licenses, Patent Pools, and Standard Setting*, *in* INNOVATION POLICY AND THE ECONOMY 119, 125 (2001).

[93] "[I]f you're selling online, at the most recent count there are 4,319 patents you could be violating. If you also planned to advertise, receive payments for, or plan shipments of your goods, you would need to be concerned with approximately 11,000." BESSEN & MEURER, *supra* note 42, at 8.

[94] FTC Report, *supra* note 4, at 51; Bessen et. al., *supra* note 13, at 34.

[95] *See* Lemley, *supra* note 90.

[96] FTC Report, *supra* note 4, at 80–90; Richard A. Posner, *Why There Are Too Many Patents in America*, THE ATLANTIC, July 12, 2012, http://www.theatlantic.com/business/archive /2012/07/why-there-are-too-many-patents-inamerica/259725/.

[97] *See, e.g.,* Bessen et. al., *supra* note 13, at 34; Posner, *supra* note 95.

[98] Allison et. al., *supra* note 7, at 708.

[99] It costs $1.5 million just to get through discovery and $2.5 million in all for suits where there is $1 million to $25 million at stake. In suits where over $25 million is at stake, it is $3 million through discovery and $5 million total. *See* AMERICAN INTELLECTUAL PROPERTY LAW ASSOCIATION, *supra* note 22.

[100] *See, e.g.,* Eon–Net LP v. Flagstar Bancorp, 653 F.3d 1314, 1326–27 (Fed. Cir. 2011) (observing that plaintiff had filed suit against 100+ defendants then quickly settled with most of them for far less than litigation costs, and the defendant who did litigate had expended $600,000 to avoid paying $25,000– $75,000 in royalties); Darren Cahr & Ira Kalina, *Of PACs and Trolls: How the Patent Wars May Be Coming to a Hospital Near You*, 19 HEALTH LAW. 15, 16 (2006) ("The patent troll offers a license for under $100,000. The end user makes a business decision—millions of dollars to defend a suit that might be lost, or $100,000 or less for certainty? The end user takes a license.").

[101] Scott A. McKeown, *USPTO to Break Patent Troll Business Model in September?*, Patents Post-Grant, http://www.patentspostgrant.com/lang/en/2012/07/patent-troll-business-model-to-change-in-september

[102] *See generally* Mark A. Lemley & Carl Shapiro, *Patent Holdup and Royalty Stacking*, 85 TEX. L. REV. 1991 (2007).

[103] *See* House ITC Hearing, *supra* note 2 (statement of Colleen V. Chien).

[104] *See* Lemley & Shapiro, *supra* note 101.

[105] *See* eBay, v. MercExchange, L.L.C., 547 U.S. 388, 391 (2006). For more information on this case, *see* CRS Report RL33429, *Availability of Injunctive Relief in Patent Cases: eBay, Inc. v. MercExchange, L.L.C.*, by Brian T. Yeh.

[106] *See eBay*, 547 U.S. at 391.

[107] The factors are: (1) necessity to prevent irreparable injury to the patent owner, (2) availability of an adequate legal remedy, such as monetary damages, (3) whether granting the injunction would be in the public interest, and (4) the balance of hardships. *See id.*

[108] See Colleen V. Chien & Mark A. Lemley, *Patent Holdup, the ITC, and the Public Interest* 10–15 (Stanford Public Law Working Paper No. 2022168, 2012); *see also* ITC House Hearing, *supra* note 2 (statement of Rep. Bob Goodlatte).

[109] U.S. INTERNATIONAL TRADE COMMISSION, FACTS AND TRENDS REGARDING USITC SECTION 337 INVESTIGATIONS (2012) http://www.usitc.gov/press_room /documents/featured_news/337facts.pdf.

[110] Chien & Lemley, *supra* note 107, at 10–15.

[111] Chien, *supra* note 67, at 1579.

[112] See Lemley & Shapiro, *supra* note 101, at 2006.

[113] P.L. 112-29 at §19; 35 U.S.C. §299; *see also* Chandran B. Iyer & Ryan M. Corbett, *Joinder Limitations in the America Invents Act: Big Change?*, ABA INTELL. PROP. LIT. COMM., February 20, 2012, *available at* http://apps.americanbar.org/litigation/committee s/intellectual/articles/winter2012-joinder-limitations-america-inventsact.html.

[114] *Id.*

[115] *See* Sheri Qualters, *'Trolls' Adapting to Limit on Multidefendant Cases,* 34 NAT'L L.J. 10 (2012).

[116] The previous version differed significantly from the current version. The SHIELD Act of 2012 (H.R. 6245) would have amended the Patent Act to provide discretionary authority for a court to award costs (including reasonable attorney's fees) to the defendant in a lawsuit alleging the infringement of a computer hardware or software patent (or in an action disputing the validity of such patent), if the court had first made a determination that the patent holder "did not have a reasonable likelihood of succeeding" in the suit. The patent owner would have been responsible for demonstrating to the court a "reasonable likelihood of succeeding" in the case to avoid potentially being required to pay the defendant's litigation costs. The bill did not define this "reasonable likelihood of succeeding" standard, however. In addition, nothing in the bill referred specifically to PAEs and thus any patent holder in an action involving a computer hardware or software patent, whether a PAE or product-producing competitor, would have been required to satisfy the new requirement.

[117] 35 U.S.C. §285.

[118] H.R. 845, §2(a), adding new section 35 U.S.C. §285A(d).

[119] *Id.* §2(a), adding new section 35 U.S.C. §285A(a)(3).

[120] *Id.* §2(a), adding new section 35 U.S.C. §285A(b).

[121] Rep. Chaffetz, *Press Release: Chaffetz, DeFazio Introduce Expanded SHIELD Act to Combat Patent Trolls,* Feb. 27, 2013, *at* http://chaffetz.house.gov/press-release/chaffetz-defazio-introduce-expanded-shield-act-combat-patenttrolls.

[122] Michael Risch, *Scratching my Head Over the SHIELD Act,* Mar. 10, 2013, *at* http://madisonian.net/2013/03/10/ scratching-my-head/.

[123] Peter Schechter, *Guest Editorial: Throwing Trolls Off the Bridge,* Mar. 10, 2013, PatentlyO Law Blog, *at* http://www.patentlyo.com/patent/2013/03/guest-editorial-throwing-trolls-off-the-bridge.html.

[124] Suits over software patents comprise 62 percent of NPE litigation, Bessen et. al., *supra* note 14, at 34, and of the most litigated patents (those litigated 8 or more times), *94 percent* were software patents. *See* Allison et. al., *supra* note 7, at 696.

[125] *See, e.g.,* Posner, *supra* note 95.

[126] Agreement on Trade-Related Aspects of Intellectual Property Rights, art. 27.1 (1994).

[127] Maria Victoria Stout, *Crossing the TRIPS Nondiscrimination Line: How CAFTA Pharmaceuticals Patent Provisions Violate TRIPS Article 27.1*,14 B.U.J. SCI. & TECH. L. 177, 181–82 (2008).

[128] *Id.* (collecting sources).

[129] Scholars have concluded that the "patent troll business model only makes economic sense when there is [substantial] inadvertent infringement." Bessen et. al., *supra* note 13, at 34.

[130] FTC Report, *supra* note 4, at 95, 102; Bessen & Meurer, *supra* note 9, at 23; Posner, *supra* note 95.

[131] FTC Report, *supra* note 4, at 95.

[132] FTC Report, *supra* note 4, at 11.

[133] FTC Report, *supra* note 4, at 101–02. The current test allows invalidation only if a claim is "insolubly ambiguous" and not subject to narrowing constructions. *Id.*

[134] FTC Report, *supra* note 4, at 102.

[135] *See* Lemley, *supra* note 12, at 630.

[136] The doctrine provides for "enhanced" damages and attorney's fees when a plaintiff shows that the infringer "acted despite objectively high likelihood that its actions constituted infringement of a valid patent." *In re* Seagate Tech., LLC, 497 F.3d 1360, 1371 (Fed. Cir. 2007) (en banc).

[137] *See* Lemley, *supra* note 12, at 631.

[138] Congress has considered legislation that would only permit plaintiffs to plead willfulness in situations where the patent "is not invalid, enforceable and has been infringed by the infringer." *See* Emily M. Van Vliet, *Patent Reform: Addressing Patent Trolling in the IT Industry While Balancing Innovation and Intellectual Property Rights*, 10 J. ENG. & PUB. POL'Y 13 (2006).

[139] The calculated risk is higher due to the enhanced damages.

[140] *See* ITC House Hearing, *supra* note 2 (statement of Colleen V. Chien).

[141] *Id.*; ITC Senate Hearing, *supra* note 2.

[142] *See* U.S. INTERNATIONAL TRADE COMMISSION, *supra* note 100.

[143] *See* Doug Lichtman & Mark A. Lemley, *Rethinking Patent Law's Presumption of Validity,* 60 STAN. L. REV. 45 (2007). Scholars say the rule has backfired and stems from an unrealistic trust in the PTO:

The theoretical justification is that patent examiners have expertise when it comes to questions of patent validity, and if patent examiners have decided that a given invention qualifies for protection, judges and juries should not second-guess the experts. But the reality is that PTO expertise is brought to bear under such poor conditions that any advantages associated with expertise are overwhelmed by the disadvantages associated where information is a natural product of the adversarial process, and where financial constraints are reduced because only a tiny fraction of all issued patents end up sufficiently valuable and contentious to warrant litigation." *Id.*

[144] 35 U.S.C. §282. For more information on the "clear and convincing evidence" standard, *see* CRS Report R41994, *The Supreme Court Decision in Microsoft v. i4i: Implications for Innovation Policy*, by John R. Thomas.

[145] *See* Lemley, *supra* note 12, at 630–31.

[146] *Id.*, at 631; Emily M. Van Vliet, *Patent Reform: Addressing Patent Trolling in the IT Industry while Balancing Innovation and Intellectual Property Rights*, 10 J. ENG. & PUB. POL'Y 15 (2006).

[147] *See* CRS Report R40481, *Patent Reform in the 111th Congress: Innovation Issues*, by Wendy H. Schacht and John R. Thomas (discussing H.R. 1260 §5(a); S. 515 §4(a); S. 610 §4(a)); CRS Report RL33996, *Patent Reform in the 110th Congress: Innovation Issues*, by John R. Thomas and Wendy H. Schacht (discussing H.R. 1908 §5(a); S. 1145 §4(a)).

[148] *Id.*

[149] Love, *supra* note 34.

[150] *Id.* at 3.

[151] "Notably, NPEs' domination of late-term litigation is almost completely attributable to firms that do nothing more than hold patents." *Id.* In other words, the "NPEs" referred to here are essentially all PAEs.

[152] *Id.*

[153] *Id.*

[154] *Id.*

[155] *Id.*

[156] *Id.* at 43 n. 156.

[157] *Id.* (citing Janice M. Mueller, *The Tiger Awakens*, 68 U. PITT. L. REV. 491, 593–97 (2007)).

[158] Marks are deemed "abandoned" under 15 U.S.C. §1127 if either of the following occurs:

(1) When its use has been discontinued with intent not to resume such use. Intent not to resume may be inferred from circumstances. Nonuse for 3 consecutive years shall be prima facie evidence of abandonment. "Use" of a mark means the bona fide use of such mark made in the ordinary course of trade, and not made merely to reserve a right in a mark.

(2) When any course of conduct of the owner, including acts of omission as well as commission, causes the mark to become the generic name for the goods or services on or in connection with which it is used or otherwise to lose its significance as a mark. Purchaser motivation shall not be a test for determining abandonment under this paragraph.

[159] This would make it easier for defendants to find relevant patents and then actually license them, which would address the issue of PAEs using shell companies and other tactics to make their patents difficult to find and license. *See* Ewing & Feldman, *supra* note 44, at 3–8.

[160] Mark A. Lemley & Nathan Myhrvold, *How to Make a Patent Market,* 20 HOFSTRA L. REV. 101 (2009).

[161] *Id.*

[162] *Id.* at 102.

[163] *Id.* at 103.

INDEX

D

H

I

J

K

L

P

Q

R

S

T

U

V

W

Y

Z